MW00479749

TGIH!
Thank God It's Heaven!

SAVORING THE JOYS OF HEAVEN TODAY AND FOREVERMORE

Samuel A. Kojoglanian, MD, FACC

TRILOGY CHRISTIAN PUBLISHERS

TUSTIN, CA

Trilogy Christian Publishers
A Wholly Owned Subsidiary of Trinity Broadcasting Network
2442 Michelle Drive
Tustin, CA 92780

Title

Copyright © 2021 by Samuel A. Kojoglanian, MD, FACC

Unless otherwise indicated, scripture taken from the New King James Version®. Copyright © 1982 by Thomas Nelson. Used by permission. All rights reserved. Emphasis added by author in parentheses.

No part of this book may be reproduced, stored in a retrieval system, or transmitted by any means without written permission from the author. All rights reserved. Printed in the USA.

Rights Department, 2442 Michelle Drive, Tustin, CA 92780.

Trilogy Christian Publishing/TBN and colophon are trademarks of Trinity Broadcasting Network.

Cover design by: Beth Harp Photography, Lagrange, Indiana

For information about special discounts for bulk purchases, please contact Trilogy Christian Publishing.

Trilogy Disclaimer: The views and content expressed in this book are those of the author and may not necessarily reflect the views and doctrine of Trilogy Christian Publishing or the Trinity Broadcasting Network.

Manufactured in the United States of America

10 9 8 7 6 5 4 3 2 1

Library of Congress Cataloging-in-Publication Data is available.

ISBN:978-1-63769-968-3

E-ISBN: 978-1-63769-969-0

Acknowledgement

Daniel and Danette Faller, who encourage continually and walk alongside loyally.

Dr. Paul Greasley, my "Bezalel," who serves faithfully and walks humbly.

Pastors Rick and Jane Kasel, who love wholeheartedly, pray earnestly, and counsel wisely.

Jeff and Denise Robertson, who care deeply, are trustworthy, and uplift graciously.

Pastor Eric Smith, who motivates fervently, protects lovingly, and sees clearly.

Dedication

To my sweet dad, Asadour Kojoglanian, who is at this very moment, enjoying the beauty of our resurrected Savior.

Foreword

Have you ever wondered what heaven is like? Is it full of cute little cherubs resting on clouds with bows and arrows? Do people recognize each other? Do all good people end up in heaven? Where is heaven? How can we make sure we go to heaven when we die? Conversely, is there really a place called hell? Is hell just a cool place to hang out with buddies and enjoy a round of golf or is hell a place of horror that should and can be avoided at all costs? This book will address these and other questions for you.

I recall the first time I stepped foot onto the University of Southern California (USC) Medical School campus. It was huge. Intimidating. I had endured a total of twenty-seven rejection letters from medical schools across America over a span of three years before gaining acceptance to USC. Sincerity did not get me in. Dreaming big did not get me in. Having good intentions did not get me in. Wanting to serve others did not get me in.

Not even my grades got me in. It was the grace of God and a competitive score on the medical college admission test that gained my acceptance. Without a respectable score, applicants cannot get into medical school no matter what their other merits.

Most would not call the rigors of medical school "heaven." In fact, many would attest that it can be "hell on earth." Likewise, heaven's "admission process" also will not look at one's sincerity, good intentions, good behavior, good giving, or good works. Gaining access to heaven has nothing to do with our accomplishments or our "test scores." In this book, *TGIH! Thank God It's Heaven*, we will investigate the requirements for getting into heaven, the joys of heaven, and the location of heaven. We will discover how heaven can transform a dull, broken life into a life of joy and goodness here on earth! Caution! We will also explore the realities of hell, the pain of hell, and the eternity of hell.

All decisions are based on facts we collect, deny, or may be ignorant of, and decisions often involve emotional choices devoid of all the facts. However, ignorance is not bliss; not only can it be deadly, but eternally deadly. Since your decisions regarding heaven and hell have eternal consequences, you will be challenged to put aside your sincerity and your good deeds and come face to face with your beliefs measured against the truth revealed in Scripture. Those beliefs will determine where you will make your eternal abode. With that in mind, let the admissions process begin!

Contents

III. Heaven Eternal

IV. Heaven Bound

I. Heaven Today

From the Church Age to the Rapture

1

Tragic Rhythm

One of the most disturbing rhythms in cardiology is called atrial fibrillation (AFib), an erratic and irregular heart rhythm that poses multiple problems for my patients from fatigue to strokes. Whether it's by simple medications or invasive means, I will do everything possible to change my patient's heart rate to a regular and controlled rhythm. In the end, however, it is not whether one has AFib or not; the real question is what caused the AFib.

One of my patients wasn't doing well and his wife called the office and begged for them come and see me. When I saw my patient, Jim, I immediately knew he was not well. I looked into his eyes; they were glazed. I took his vitals; his blood pressure was elevated. I listened to his lungs; the breath sounds were diminished. I placed the stethoscope upon his heart; it was erratic and fast. I knew he was in AFib and to verify it, I did an electrocardiogram which confirmed the diagnosis.

Direct questions were asked. Has anything changed in the diet? No. Has anything changed at home? No. Has the salt intake increased? No. Has he started drinking again? No. Has he been taking his medications? Yes, yes, an unwavering yes!

"Be serious with me, Jim, have you been taking your medications as prescribed...faithfully?"

"Well," Jim said sheepishly; he looked down and continued, "I guess I haven't been taking the medications as you told me to."

"Okay, let's go over the medications one by one," I suggested. He hadn't been taking three of his pills. One of them was the most important, as he had a heart attack in the past and I had opened up his heart arteries with stents.

"Why didn't you take the medications, Jim?"

"I just didn't feel like it," he admitted.

His wife hit him on the chest and said, "And now you tell us?"

"How long have you been doing this, Jim?" I asked.

"Oh, about a month or so," he admitted.

I strongly advised Jim to go to the hospital. He refused. He didn't appreciate that he was a very sick man. I instructed him on how to take the medications and gave him an appointment to see me in the same week. Twenty-four hours later, I received a strange phone call. It was a sheriff asking if I would sign a death certificate.

"On whom?" I asked. On my patient, Jim, who snubbed the notion of going to the hospital, and the next day he died at home.

Tragic! Tragic in more ways than one. Not only did I lose a patient, but for many years I had talked to Jim about Jesus Christ and how much Christ loved him. I told Jim that Jesus left heaven to come to earth just for him, sharing how all of humanity is born in sin and how we have fallen short of God's glory. I would joke with him and tell him that Jesus' blood type was "D."

"D?" Jim asked, looking at me funny.

"Yup!" I'd say, "You know our blood type is either A, B, AB or O, but Jesus...He has D...D for Divine!" He would laugh and we would enjoy our times together. I would continue to tell him how deeply Christ loved him; how

He gave up His life just for him, dying on the cross; how He was raised from the grave on the third day; and how He wanted to be Jim's Savior, healer, and helper.

Jim was an intellectual man with a keen mind, but he did not believe in Christ or His atoning blood. He thought of himself as a good man, and he was. He thought of himself as a good husband, and he was. He thought of himself as a good dad, and he was. He thought of himself as a good friend, and he was.

I signed his death certificate. We know where his body went: into a coffin. But where did his soul and spirit go? If he did not go to heaven, where did he end up, and is it possible to pray him out of oblivion and into heaven? Did he open his eyes to witness God's glory, and to bask in the Lord's beauty? Did he begin worshiping the Savior wholeheartedly, singing, "TGIH! Thank God It's Heaven," in God's breathtaking assembly? Or did he open his eyes in pain, tragically, helplessly, and sadly suffering in hades, a holding place for unbelievers, before ending up in hell eternally?

One wrong decision caused his physical death.
One tragic choice decided his eternal destiny.
May I ask?
Where has the joy gone from your life?

What decision are you making today regarding your eternity?

And where will you go after your last breath?

2

Nine Hours, Six Trials, One Cross

Everyone longs to go to heaven and delight in its joys, but the question is who will make it in, and who will be denied? I have learned much about heaven in the strangest place: at the tomb of Christ. You may find that odd as well but join me as we take a journey with one of Christ's most beloved disciples, Mary Magdalene (John 20:11–18).

On Friday, the most horrid day of the Passion Week, Jesus was betrayed by Judas and faced six illegal trials, three by the Jews and three by the Gentiles. It all started with a kiss of betrayal in the Garden of Gethsemane and led to the cross on the hills of Calvary. These events all took place within a record-breaking time of nine hours. The Sanhedrin, the Supreme Court of the Jews, declared Christ guilty of blasphemy before He even set foot into their court. Pilate, the Roman governor, knew

He was innocent, but to appease the Jewish leaders and save his career, he succumbed and gave Jesus up to be slaughtered by crucifixion on a rugged wooden cross. Jesus was brutally beaten; the Bible states that He was unrecognizable, "His visage was marred more than any man. And His form more than the sons of men" (Isa. 52:14). How could that be? He was marred beyond recognition not only because He endured physical brutality, but He also bore all the sins of mankind in His own body (1 Peter 2:24).

Do you ever wonder how the hills of Calvary were chosen by the Romans as the site for many crucifixions? Was it random? Was it strategic? Was it convenient? This was not just any hill or mountain. It was chosen in the outskirts of Jerusalem so that those who walked by could hurl insults at the criminals hanging on the crosses. However, even if it were strategically chosen, those who used the hill likely had no idea of its significance.

Calvary was the same place as Mount Moriah, where Abraham came to sacrifice his son Isaac 2,000 years before (Gen. 22:1–19). But God intervened and provided an unblemished ram. It was the exact hill where David made his sacrifice to stop the plague in Israel (2 Sam. 24:1–25). Traditionally, it was the same place where David buried the head of the giant Goliath. And it would become the exact same hill where Jesus would crush the head of Satan (Gen. 3:15). Just as God provided a means for Isaac to live, and just as God poured out mercy on David and Israel to stop the plague, so too God allowed His Son to die on the cross to take away your sin and my sin.

The death of Jesus Christ was brutal; He received thirty-nine beatings on His back with a cruel leather whip with embedded metal pieces, followed by His suffering the cross where He died physically. His body was then taken to Joseph of Arimathea's tomb on Friday evening, right before sundown (Mark 15:42).

Our story takes place three days later, the Sunday of His resurrection. The only people that knew of the supernatural resurrection were the Roman soldiers who were guarding the tomb. They were placed there so none of Christ's disciples could possibly steal His body and later claim that He had been raised from the dead (Matt. 27:62–66).

God's glory shook the earth, and the Roman soldiers fell as if they were dead, the stone was moved by an angel of the Lord and Jesus rose from the grave in His glorified body (Matt. 28:1–3). Can you imagine the scene? Overwhelming!

A Roman soldier would not dare go to sleep on his watch. First, the Roman seal was placed over the tomb. The seal was a sign of authentication that the tomb was occupied, and the power and authority of Rome stood behind the seal. Anyone found breaking the Roman seal would suffer an unpleasant death. Second, Scripture favors the tomb being guarded by an elite Roman guard which consisted of a sixteen-man unit. Each member was responsible for six square feet of space. None were allowed to sit down or lean against anything while they were on duty. If a guard fell asleep, he was beaten to death and burned. But he would not be the only one executed; the entire sixteen-man unit would be executed because of the mistake of one! And is it possible that all these Roman soldiers fell asleep while the disciples of Christ came to steal the body? Not a chance! But the stone was rolled away, and the tomb was empty!

3

Little Love, Much Love

Early Sunday morning, the ladies who loved Jesus, including Mary Magdalene and Mary the mother of Jesus, came to the tomb where Jesus had been laid on Friday evening, but miraculously found that it was empty. Mary Magdalene ran to tell Peter and John; both men ran to the tomb and witnessed Jesus' body garment intact and head garment folded, without the body of Jesus being present (John 20:1–10).

All went back home except Mary Magdalene. She lingered, wondering what to do, and perhaps, hoping to find the body of Jesus. She loved Him much. Why? Because she had been forgiven much, as Jesus had cast out seven demons from her body. Jesus gives us the secret of love in Luke 7:36–50: to whom little is forgiven, the same loves little; to whom much is forgiven, the same loves much.

Mary Magdalene was forgiven of much; therefore, she loved Jesus much. How much do you love Jesus? Do you love Him more today than you did yesterday? I am not asking about lip service. I am not asking about knee service. I am not even asking about church and community service. I am asking about your heart service. Many are bending the knee, but not bending the heart. Where do you and I stand? It's worth knowing the answer, don't you think?

What Mary Magdalene saw was heaven on earth. Come and enter the tomb with me and witness the joy of heaven and the glory of God!

4

Two Angels, One Sacrifice

As Mary Magdalene continued to mourn, she stooped down and looked into the tomb. What she saw must have been baffling! The linen cloths, in which Jesus was buried, were there in the form of His body but without Jesus. The linen handkerchief that was around His head was folded where His head was lying earlier that day. But He was not there!

She then saw two angels in white sitting, one at the head and the other at the feet, where the body of Jesus had lain. Jesus' burial clothes were there, but He was missing. The angels were sitting on the stone slab upon which the body of Christ rested for three days. In between the two angels was the blood-stained clothing of Christ.

What did Mary Magdalene really see? If we were to flash back to approximately 1500 BC, we, along with Mary Magdalene, would witness what Moses saw in the tabernacle's Holy of Holies: the ark of the covenant upon which God's glory and presence resided. Moses led about three million Israelites out of the grips of Pharaoh. What was supposed to be a ten to eleven-day journey to the Promised Land, turned into a forty-year lengthy ordeal. During the forty-year wilderness journey, Moses was instructed to build a tabernacle where the presence of God would reside among His people.

The tabernacle had an outer court where innocent animals were slain, and the spilled blood would atone for the sins of the people. The priests would then go into the Holy Place where the golden table of shewbread, the golden lampstand, and the golden altar of incense were located. Only the high priest was allowed once a year to enter the Holy of Holies, where the ark of the covenant was housed and where God's glory was present. The ark contained the ten commandments, Aaron's rod, and the manna, representing God's statutes, God's chosen leader and God's provision, respectively (Heb. 9:4).

There was much complaining, fretting, and unbelieving during the journey. Psalm 37:8–9 warns us that fretting and unbelief lead to evil. What do we hear in heaven? Complaints? Moaning? Sighing? Grumbling?

No. None of the above. The language of heaven is worship. Worthy is the Lamb of God who was slain! Glory, glory, hallelujah!

We are encouraged to worship and praise God while in our earthly tents: "Rejoice always, pray without ceasing. In everything give thanks for this is the will of God in Christ Jesus for you" (1 Thess. 5:16–18). We also read in Psalm 70:4, "Let all those who seek You rejoice and be glad in You and let those who love Your salvation say continually, 'Let God be magnified!'" I pray that even in our pain, our hearts burst forth with worshiping our Lord, our God, our Christ, our Savior! Yes, even in our pain, we can go to God's throne of grace, obtaining mercy and enjoying His presence!

During Moses' days, the high priest, Aaron, entered the Holy of Holies on the annual Day of Atonement, and sprinkled the blood of an innocent young bull on the Mercy Seat, the covering of the ark. The Mercy Seat had two golden angels on top. When God saw the blood, He accepted it as an atonement for the sins of the people. The high priest would then come out into the courtyard where the people waited and proclaim, "Forgiven!" The Israelites would rejoice, knowing their sins were forgiven for another year. Could Mary Magdalene have been looking into Jesus' empty tomb, and seeing the Mercy Seat and the ark of the covenant?

5

Draw Me Nearer

If we were to flash forward from the tabernacle to the cross and to the empty tomb, we'd see the perfect sacrifice, Jesus Christ, slain for the sin of the world. We find in 1 John 4:10 that, "This is love, not that we loved God but that He loved us and sent His only Son as a propitiation for our sins." The word "propitiation" is a big word for atonement or a payment that satisfies, meaning Jesus paid in full the price for our sins. In the Greek, "propitiation" is *hilasmos*, the exact word for Mercy Seat! Amazing! Jesus Christ is the Mercy Seat!

When God looked down and saw the perfect sacrifice of His Son, He accepted it as a payment for our sins. What Mary saw in the tomb were two angels and a stone slab stained with the blood of the perfect Lamb of God. The two angels, one seated on one end and the other at the opposite end, looked down at the blood-stained slab cover of the Mercy Seat, a striking depiction of the ark of the covenant. "The Lord reigns; let the peoples tremble! He dwells between the cherubim; let the earth be moved" (Ps. 99:1).

Forgiven, forgiven! Sin debt cancelled! Those who come to the Mercy Seat of Christ will be forgiven forevermore! (Eph. 1:7).

The high priest had to enter the Holy of Holies every year with a sacrifice. Jesus was crucified only once. The high priest had to make a sacrifice for his own sins. Jesus is sinless and is the perfect sacrifice. The blood of animals covered the sins of the people, and that is why the high priest had to enter the Holy of Holies time and time again. The blood of Christ completely and eternally cleanses the sins of all those who come to Him. Christ, the Great High Priest, will never be crucified again; He is forever glorified and is worthy of all honor and praise! (Heb. 9:6–7, 23–28).

God provided for Himself a lamb just as Abraham had prophesied in 1900 BC (Gen. 22:8). After His death, Jesus Christ did not enter the Holy Place made by human hands, but heaven itself, to appear in the presence of God and make intercession for us (Heb. 9:24–25). Those of us who love Him are welcome to enter the Holy of Holies daily as intentional followers of Jesus Christ, and experience the glory, the beauty, and the joys of knowing God today!

When Jesus died on the cross, the veil that separated the ark of the covenant from all the people was ripped from top to bottom, indicating God ripped it from above. Because the veil is torn, we have direct access to enter heaven right now! Jesus Christ is the Great High Priest who sympathizes with our weaknesses, knowing our limitations and the trials we face. We can, therefore, "come boldly to the throne of grace, that we may obtain mercy and find grace to help in time of need" (Heb. 4:16).

Why then don't we more often figuratively enter heaven before we even get there? The nearer we draw to the cross, the more we magnify Jesus Christ and minimize our problems. The nearer we draw to the cross, the more freely we enter the throne of grace finding fellowship with the Father. The nearer we draw to the cross, the more we will fulfill and enjoy the hope of our calling. The nearer we draw to the cross, the more we will experience the same resurrection power that raised Jesus Christ from the dead, finding sufficient strength for every problem.

Can it really be that simple? Can we really change water into wine as Jesus did in Cana of Galilee? (John 2:1–10). Can we really transform from the dull, insipid, mundane, angry, scared, lonely, and broken beings into servants of the Most High God, laughing, believing, caring, hoping, enjoying, supernaturally achieving, and carrying out the will of God here on earth? Can we walk in God's heavenly glory today? Yes! Yes!

The nearer we draw to the cross, the more we will enjoy the riches of God's glory. The nearer we draw to the cross, the more we will soar on the wings of eagles, run and not be weary, walk and not faint (Isa. 40:31). The nearer we draw to the cross, the more we will experience great and perfect peace, even during turmoil, disasters, hardships, and pandemics (Isa. 26:3; Ps. 119:165). The nearer we draw to the cross, the more we will be aware of our status...we are saved by grace and sit together in the heavenly places in Christ Jesus, enjoying his mercy, kindness, love, and favor. (Eph. 1:17–20; 2:6–7). Yes, all of God's goodness and more, today!

The nearer we draw to God's Word, the clearer we see heaven, and experience God's compassions and tender mercies today. The Word is clear in Ephesians 2:6: that God has raised us up with Christ and seated us together in the heavenly places in Christ Jesus (now).

The nearer we draw into God's courts with singing, joyful shouts, gladness, thanksgiving and praise, the more we will savor the presence of the living God (Ps. 100).

I believe we are trying to obtain the glories of heaven by committing our lives to acquire status, possessions, and positions on earth. A small adjustment will drastically change everything in our lives. Let's draw closer to the cross, committing ourselves to God's Word, not because we follow the letter of God's law but because we respond to the goodness of God's love. We will then not only obtain the glories of heaven, but our broken vessels will supernaturally change into wells of living waters! Yes, today!

6

Enjoying More of Heaven Now

It is often believed that eternal life begins after physical death. Jesus defined eternal life clearly for us in John 17:3, "And this is eternal life, that they (Christ followers) may know You (God, the Father), the only true God, and Jesus Christ whom You have sent." Eternal life does not start after death. It begins the moment one accepts Christ as Savior and Lord. Eternal life is not knowing about God as so many do; it is to know God, love Him, adore Him, delight in Him, commit to Him, desire to spend time with Him, and bask in His love for you!

When God's will becomes our will and when our hearts' desires become knowing God, then our perception will change, our anxiety will decrease, our fears will subside, our heartaches will be cured, our minds will be at peace, and we will begin enjoying heaven today and now!

According to Psalm 16:11, "There is fullness of joy in God's presence, and pleasures at His right hand forevermore." Can you or I really say that we are experiencing "fullness of joy" today? I pray you are, even amid your pain, hardships, losses, grieving, and setbacks. "That's impossible!" you may object. You are absolutely right… if we have our eyes, ears, minds, and hearts set upon the promises of this world. But when we delight in the Lord today and make Him the very desire of our hearts, then what seems impossible, enjoying heaven today, becomes very possible!

If enjoying heaven is not real for us today, then we may want to consider why we came to Christ. Many come to Him to escape hell, which is obviously given to those who accept Him as a gift of His atonement! Once that is settled, the thorns and worries of life seem to choke the presence, goodness, joy of knowing God, and fellowshipping with Him day to day.

We face disappointments, despair, and depression because we care so much about ourselves, indulging ourselves in the bottomless pit of self. When we see our wishes denied and our egos bruised, we are devastated! Many of us are not content because we care about ourselves disproportionally, and care about God's kingdom meagerly.

Moreover, many Christ followers are ignorant of the benefits of salvation:

1. Being saved.
2. Being healed.
3. Being set free of mental oppression, depression, and satanic strongholds.
4. Being set free from a pauper's mentality.

Some may object, but we will let Scripture support each of the four attributes of salvation:

1. Isaiah 53:5 and 1 Peter 2:24 describe how Jesus took on all our sins in His body on the cross so that we may become righteous, "He was wounded for our transgressions, He was bruised for our iniquities." According to Ephesians 1:7, "In Him (Jesus Christ) we have redemption through His blood, the forgiveness of sins, according to the riches of His grace." God did not send His Son to condemn us, but to save us (John 3:17). According to John 10:28, Jesus gives us eternal life and we shall never perish, nor can anyone snatch us out of His hand.

2. Isaiah 53:5 and 1 Peter 2:24 also teach us that God gave us the gift of healing (by His stripes we have

become healed). His Word has gone forth and it brings healing and saves us from destruction, according to Psalm 107:20. According to Psalm 103:3, the "package" of salvation is not only that God forgives us all our sins, but He also heals us of all our diseases. Proverbs 4:20–22 directs us to His Word, which brings life and healing to the whole body. Jeremiah 30:17 states that the Lord will restore our health and heal our wounds. Jesus healed all those who came to Him (Luke 4:40); you will never hear or read an account where Jesus made anyone sick! It is God's will for you to be well, whole, and healed (3 John 1:2).

3. Isaiah 53:5 further shows us that His punishment produces peace of mind. We also turn to Acts 10:38 which tells us that God anointed Jesus with the Holy Spirit to heal those under the power of the devil. In Luke 8:26–39, we read that when Jesus stepped out of the boat in the region of Gadarenes, He was met by a demon-possessed man. Jesus cast a legion of demons out of him, and those who came by, witnessed that the man was sitting at the feet of Jesus, clothed, and in the right frame of mind! In Philippians 4:5–6, Paul encourages us not to be anxious about anything but to pray, be thankful and make our requests

known unto God. Why are Christ followers anxious and why do we lack a peace of mind? If I dare say, many of us don't pray nor are we very thankful! The mind is where all your battles are fought. If Satan has occupied your mind, he has nabbed your soul and has stolen your peace!

4. Finally, in some circles, it is considered spiritual if Christ followers remain poor. There is nothing in Scripture that supports this notion. In 2 Corinthians 8:9, we read that Christ, though He was rich, became poor for our sakes, that we, through His poverty, may become rich. In Psalm 92:12, we read, "The righteous shall flourish like a palm tree." Proverbs 10:22 declares, "The blessing of the Lord makes one rich, and He adds no sorrow with it," and 3 John 1:2 states, "Beloved, I pray that you may prosper in all things and be in health, just as your soul prospers."

All this may be new to a Christ-follower who is feeling condemned, broken, depressed, hopeless, and broke. How then can our hearts get back into a healthy rhythm, being one with our Father, enjoying heaven now?

By reading the books of Psalms and Chronicles we find that an integral way of enjoying heaven right now entails praising God, "Give unto the Lord the glory due to His name. Worship the Lord in the beauty of holiness. Oh, magnify the Lord with me and let us exalt His name together. Sing praises to God, sing praises! Sing praises to our King, sing praises! For God is the King of all the earth. Sing to Him a psalm of praise! Great is the Lord, and greatly to be praised in the city of our God, in His holy mountain. I will praise the name of God with a song and will magnify Him with thanksgiving. Praise the Lord! Praise God in His sanctuary; praise Him in His mighty heavens! Praise Him for His mighty acts; praise Him according to His excellent greatness! Give to the Lord, O families of the peoples, give to the Lord glory and strength. Give to the Lord the glory due His name; bring an offering and come before Him. Oh, worship the Lord in the beauty of holiness!" (Ps. 29:2; 34:3; 47:6–7; 48:1; 69:30; 150:1–2; 1 Chron. 16:28–29).

There is a second key element which will help us savor the joys of heaven today. It is not found in entertainment, which has become an addiction for so many, including the church goer. Masses are expecting to find an escape, a diversion, and a lasting happiness in the world of entertainment. The second key element is also not found in education, possessions, nor positions, which can take a lifetime to obtain and lead us to the dead-end street of emptiness. What then is the key? It is hope. Hebrews 10:23 heartens us, "Let us hold fast the confession of our hope without wavering, for He who promised is faithful." Biblical hope is not the same as worldly hope, or lack of assurance that says, "I hope so." Biblical hope is a confident assurance and anticipation of God's promises being fulfilled (Heb. 11:1).

As water is crucial for the body to live, so too is hope vital for the soul to thrive. However, hope's chief rival is despair. Once despair grips the heart of the Christ-follower, it chokes the breath out of his soul, snatches away all assurance, imprisons his joy, and robs him of any goodness. Hope brings gladness (Prov. 10:28). Hope renews (Isa. 40:31). Hope gives purpose (Jer. 29:11). Hope makes all things possible in Christ (Mark 9:23). Hope does not put us to shame (Rom. 5:5). Hope takes our eyes off our circumstances and places our eyes on God (Ps. 33:22). As we wait upon the Lord, our blessed hope is the imminent appearing of our great God and Savior, Jesus Christ (Titus 2:13)!

Faith, allied closely to hope, is yet another essential factor to savor in the joys of heaven daily. "Now faith is the substance of things hoped for and the evidence of things not seen. But without faith it is impossible to please God, for he who comes to Him must believe that

He is, and that He is a rewarder of those who diligently seek Him" (Heb. 11:1, 6).

Faith provides evidence of the invisible domain without using the five senses of seeing, smelling, tasting, hearing, and touching. It offers proof of things that are undetectable in the physical world and immeasurable in the scientist's test tube. Abraham "waited for the city which has foundations, whose builder and maker is God" (Heb. 11:10). Abraham did not see heaven with his eyes but believed by faith in the coming of the new heaven known as the new Jerusalem. According to Hebrews 11:39–40, the Old Testament saints were commended for their faith yet none of them received what had been promised to them. There is coming a day when the Old and the New Testament saints will rejoice together in perfect hope, perfect joy, perfect love, in a perfect place...in the presence of our Lord Jesus Christ!

Here are the keys to experiencing more of heaven today. Praise, hope, and faith! With these God-given gifts, we are encouraged to make God the desire of our hearts and Christ the reason for our living. This feat is made possible only when we spend quality time in the Word (Psalm 1), cancelling out ignorance (2 Cor. 2:11), communing with our Lord God (1 Cor. 1:9; Rev. 3:20), understanding the benefits of walking with the Lord

(Ps. 103:1–5), and allowing the Holy Spirit to teach us all things (John 14:26). Only then can we taste the goodness of the Lord, and step into the joy of His presence...even at this very moment!

A word of caution. Unbelief cancels out praise, smothers hope, and ravages faith. The disciples of Christ, who were given the power to heal all kinds of disease and cast out unclean spirits, and were successful, failed to do so when it came to an epileptic child (Matt. 10:1–8; Luke 10:1–20; Matt. 17:16). Why? Did they not have faith? It had nothing to do with their faith. Jesus said, "If you have faith as a mustard seed, you will say to this mountain, 'Move from here to there,' and it will move, and nothing will be impossible for you" (Matt. 17:20). The disciples had already exercised their faith and successfully healed multitudes according to Luke 10. In the same verse we find that Jesus identifies the reason for their failure: unbelief. Faith propels us heavenward. Unbelief drives us to become aware of what we see, hear, taste, feel and smell, and therefore makes us self-conscious instead of God-conscious.

You and I don't need "huge" faith...all we need is faith as small as a mustard seed! What we need is to get rid of our unbelief so that we may start savoring in the joys of heaven today. How can we increase our belief and decrease or even eliminate our unbelief? Jesus gives us the answer in Matthew 17:22: through prayer and fasting. Enjoying heaven on earth is not passively obtained. It requires effort on our part, daily, consistently, and faithfully.

Anyone can "believe"; even the demons believe in God and tremble (James 2:19). Believing is not singing Christian lyrics, tattooing the body with a verse, or doing God a favor by reading a five-minute devotional. Believing is committing our lives to God, praying continually, rejoicing always, and giving thanks to Him in all circumstances. Believing is not a three-step, seven-step, or twelve-step program. Believing is letting God, the person of Christ, the very Word, live in our hearts through the power of the Holy Spirit.

Aren't you tired of the ordinary? It is time to rise! It is time to change this routine stagnant life of ours into supernatural waters bursting out of our hearts! It is time to enjoy heaven on earth...today!

7

Most Beautiful Word in the Bible

The two angels in the tomb asked Mary Magdalene why she was weeping. She said, "They have taken away my Lord, and I do not know where they have laid Him" (John 20:13). She did not know who "they" were and neither do we, but we do know that no one took Him, for no one and nothing would be able "to take" or "take on" the Son of God! Jesus Christ alone conquered death and the grave!

Mary Magdalene then turned around and saw Jesus standing outside the tomb, but she did not recognize Him. Jesus said to her, "Woman, why are you weeping? Whom are you seeking?" (John 20:15). I often jest that when Jesus spoke these words, it was the first recorded rap song in the history of mankind: "Why you weeping? Who you seeking?"

Because she thought that He was the gardener, she begged Him to tell her where Jesus' body had been taken. She loved Him much and wanted to protect Him. Given that she was asking for His body, it becomes obvious that she did not realize that He was risen from the dead. In her grief, this notion was beyond her imagination.

Jesus speaks one of the most beautiful words recorded in the Bible. I love what He says in John 20:16. It's just a simple word, just one word, but Jesus' lips are drenched with grace and goodness. What would He say that would amaze and take her breath away? What would He say that would affect her so deeply? What would He say that would touch her soul and ease her pain?

He simply spoke one word, "Mary." Please don't miss this. He was not just calling out her name. He spoke in the gentlest voice and in that one word, "Mary," are hidden treasures.

I hear Jesus saying, "Mary, I have loved you before the foundations of the world; I knitted you together in your mother's womb and you are fearfully and wonderfully made; I freed you of your bondages and saved you from destruction; I was slain so you may have salvation and an abundant life; you are the joy of my heart, and I have called you My own!" (Eph.1:4; Ps. 139:13–14; Ps. 103:4; Rev. 5:9; John 10:10; 1 John 3:1).

"Mary, you are My friend, My child, My beloved, the apple of My eye, and I treasure you and hold you dear to my heart" (Ps. 17:8; Songs 2:4).

"Mary, I love you with an everlasting love, I will crown your head with my lovingkindness and tender mercies and feed you with good mercies and unending favor" (Ps. 103:4–5).

"Mary, I died for you so that you may live in hope and not in despair!" (2 Cor. 4:8).

"Mary, I AM the bread of life; taste and see that I am good; you shall never go hungry; you shall never thirst; you shall live and not die" (John 6:35, 48; Ps. 34:8; Ps. 118:17).

"Mary, I AM the light of the world; if you follow Me, you shall never walk in the darkness; even if you walk through the most difficult hardships, I will walk with you, I will carry you, and I will sustain you for I AM the light of life" (John 8:12, 9:5; Ps. 55:22; 119:116, 175; Isa. 46:4).

"Mary, I AM the gate; if you enter through Me, you shall be saved; you shall be safe; you shall be secure; you shall find green pastures; you shall find perfect peace; you shall find your true purpose; you shall find life" (John 10:9; Ps. 23:2; Isa. 26:3; Rom. 12:1–2).

"Mary, I AM the Good Shepherd; I laid down My life for the sheep; I laid down my life for you; I will not allow the crooked shepherds to snatch you out of My loving hands" (John 10:11, 28–29; Zech. 11:15–16).

"Mary, I AM the resurrection and the life; death has no grip on Me; those who believe in Me, though they die, yet shall they live. Mary, I sacrificed my life for you so that you may live; I live so you may rise" (John 11:25; Acts 2:24).

"Mary, I AM the way, the truth and the life; come to Me for I am the only way to the Father who loves you, calls you by name, and will always walk with you. Mary, My love for you is forever...I love you with an everlasting love!" (John 14:6; Acts 4:12; Jer. 31:3).

"Mary, I AM the vine, you are the branch; remain in Me as I remain in you; for in Me you will bear much fruit; with my love, you will be able to bear all things, believe

all things, hope in all things, and endure all things"
(John 15:1–5; 1 Cor. 13:7).

"Mary!"

8

If You Can't See, Listen

If you were to hear Jesus speak your name instead of "Mary," you would hear the Lord Jesus say to you, "I will never leave you.

I will never disown you.

I will never abandon you.

I will never hurt you.

I will never neglect you.

I will never sabotage you.

I will never forsake you.

I will never divorce you.

I will carry you when you cannot walk.

I will honor you when you are belittled.

I will welcome you when you are rejected.

I will comfort you when you are broken.

I will defend you when you are mistreated.

I will mend you when you are hurting.

I will heal you when you are sick.

I'm not only preparing a place for you, but I'm interceding with My Father and your Father on your behalf.

Come, though your sins are like scarlet, I will make you white as snow.

Come, though your wounds are deep and raw, I will anoint you with My healing balm.

Come, though your past shames you, I will remove your sins and the guilt of your sins from you, and fill your heart with joy.

Come, though your friends and family may forsake you, I will never leave you.

Come, and see the glory of heaven in Me, for I AM Immanuel, God with you!"

(Deut. 31:6; Josh.1:5; Heb.10:22; 13:5; Luke 18:16; Isa. 1:18–19; Isa. 43:18–19; Isa. 7:14).

If you are on the verge of giving up, please stop for a moment and listen. If you are literally on the verge of ending your life, put that weapon down once and for all, and listen. If you are hopeless, lend me your ears and listen intently. Whatever you have done; whatever you have said; whatever has been done and said to you; whatever horror, loss, shame, or guilt you may be facing, there is One who walks by your side, who knows how to pick you up, strengthen you, guide you, instruct you, counsel you, teach you, honor you, love you and watch over you! Please, do not give up. Please, look up. Don't give up...

look up! Where does your help come from? Your help "Comes from the Lord, who made heaven and earth. He will not allow your foot to be moved; He who keeps you will not slumber. The Lord shall preserve your going out and your coming from this time forth and even forevermore" (Ps. 121:2-3, 8). He is your Redeemer and the lover of your soul!

Who is this Jesus? He is the Creator Jesus. He is the Crucified Jesus. He is the Conquering Jesus. He is the Comforting Jesus. He is the Compassionate Jesus. He is the Coming Jesus! Mary Magdalen turned to Him and said, "Rabboni!" She saw Him as the Teacher of teachers, the Rabbi of rabbis, the Healer of healers, the God of all gods!

Notice that when she was looking for Him, she did not find Him. But when she heard Him, she found her Christ. If you are looking for Jesus, but cannot find Him, listen to His Word and you shall find Him. His gentle voice will beckon you, saying, "Come to Me, all you who labor and are heavy laden, and I will give you rest" (Matt. 11:28). Come. Come if you are weary. Come if you have failed. Come if you are facing defeat. Come if you have given up. Come and find rest; come and find hope; come and find joy; come and experience heaven on earth for your hurting soul!

9

Is Jesus a Liar?

Mary exclaimed, "Rabboni!" The word *rabboni* means the "master of rabbis." Jesus then said something to her that for years I could not understand, "Do not cling to Me for I have not yet ascended to My Father, but go to My brethren and say to them, 'I am ascending to my Father and your Father, and to My God and your God'" (John 20:17).

How could Jesus say that He had not yet ascended to heaven to His Father? We find in Luke 23:43 that Jesus told the thief on the cross, "Today you will be with Me in Paradise." He said, "today," meaning Friday, the day of His crucifixion. We also find in Luke 23:46 that when He was dying, He proclaimed, "Father, into Your hands I commit my spirit." He committed His spirit at the point of His death. In our story, Jesus is speaking to Mary Magdalene three days later, on Sunday, the resurrection day, and He is telling her that He has not yet ascended to the Father.

Is Jesus Christ a con artist? Is He a mad man? Or is He who He says He is, the Resurrection and the Life? (John 11:25). It is here that we must answer the critic and the skeptic who claim that there are inconsistencies in the Bible. I believe the Bible is the Word of God; it is God's voice; it is Jesus Christ, the Logos, God who became flesh. I also believe that the Bible is infallible, inerrant, indestructible, instructional, profitable, unbreakable, and eternal.

If we look at a human being, all we see is height, weight, facial features, hair color, clothing, age, and gender. Would you agree that we spend an enormous amount of time in making ourselves presentable? Get in shape. Smile pretty. Stand up tall. Speak with confidence. But that is not the real you. It is not the real me. We spend most of the day "looking in the mirror," feeding ourselves, getting rest, and working. However, the real person is not only the body, the physical being, but consists of the soul and the spirit, both being separate entities and both being eternal. In 1 Thessalonians 5:23, the apostle Paul gives us insight about our triune nature, "Now may the God of Peace Himself sanctify you completely; and may your spirit, soul, and body be preserved blameless at the coming of our Lord Jesus Christ."

The soul is one's personality, mind (the brain), emotions, and will; it tells us if we are happy or sad, angry or at peace, scared or courageous. The soul can be manipulated by simple words or actions. For instance, if someone were to cut into "your" lane on the freeway, you may get angry.

The spirit is the part of us where God communicates; it is where God's life, breath, and power flow; it is not influenced by our senses (what we see, hear, taste, smell and touch). It cannot be seen or felt; if we are bought by the blood of the Lamb, it is the part of us that is a new creation, born again, completely righteous and sealed by the Holy Spirit (2 Cor. 5:17, 21; Eph. 1:13). We read in 1 John 3:9, "Whoever has been born of God does not sin, for His seed remains in him; and he cannot sin, because he has been born of God." Christ followers are born of God but do commit sins. Then, is the Bible wrong? God forbid! Our spirit, born of God, cannot sin and will never sin! It is our souls (physical minds) and bodies that sin.

Once we agree that we are hopelessly born in sin, desperately needing the atoning blood of Jesus Christ, and admitting that we are in a spiritually "erratic and tragic rhythm," then we receive a new spirit that is sealed and controlled by the Holy Spirit. The spirit is the only part of a believer's life that is currently and completely saved, not needing to "mature" or grow, and it will not undergo change when we get to heaven! Our spirit, found in Christ and made new by His atoning blood, is singing and dancing in complete health, complete joy, complete goodness, and complete hope. It is singing, "TGIH! Hallelujah! Praises to our God! I am a new creation, and I'll shout it from the mountain tops, 'Thank God It's Heaven!'"

On the other hand, the soul, our mind, is desperately trying to decide whether to follow our new spirit or the physical sensual world. Our minds can be and should be continually renewed by God's Word (Rom. 12:1–2; Ps. 19:7). We wholeheartedly desire for our soul to have the pure attitude and righteousness of the Spirit of God in our earthly journey but seem to fall short daily. There is hope! The more we saturate ourselves in God's Word, the more our mind will be influenced by our spirit, translating into a life of love, joy, peace, patience, kindness, goodness, faithfulness, gentleness, and self-control! (Gal. 5:16, 22–23). Even a greater reality is that the soul will one day be completely transformed in heaven! Hallelujah!

Though we desperately try to stop the body from aging, it is this earthly tent that gradually "matures." The real person is the spirit and the soul, both that will live for all eternity. As we will later discuss in chapters fifteen and twenty-seven, the body will also be changed. For the believer, it will be glorified, leading to eternal life; for the unbeliever, it will be become dishonored, culminating in eternal death.

If Jesus ascended into heaven on Friday after His death, why would He tell Mary Magdalene otherwise? He did ascend to heaven...but in His soul and spirit. "For Christ also suffered once for sins, the righteous for the unrighteous, to bring you to God. He was put to death in the body but made alive in the Spirit" (1 Peter 3:18). Therefore, as He was talking with Mary, He had not yet ascended into heaven in His glorified body, which would take place forty days after His resurrection.

There is no mystery or contradiction here for the skeptic to claim that Jesus was a liar. He told Mary Magdalen the truth because Jesus is the truth!

1 0

Preaching to the "Dead"

When did Jesus ascend to heaven? On the day of His death. Before ascending to heaven, however, Jesus first visited hades (Sheol in Hebrew and *hades* in Greek). Hades, as we will read below, is a horrid place, occupied by the souls and spirits of those who disdain God, reject Christ and mock the Holy Spirit.

What is hades and is it the same as hell? Hades and hell are two different dwellings, both tragically hopeless destinations, but hades is temporary and in the depths of the earth, and hell is permanent and in outer darkness. Hades has two parts. The side of torment is where the souls and spirts of unbelievers who have physically died throughout history are housed awaiting judgment at the Great White Throne before being sent to eternal hell. The paradise side, or Abraham's bosom, is where the souls and spirits of believers went at the moment of their death who died before the resurrection of Jesus.

After the cross, the souls from the paradise side were taken up to heaven by Jesus, and now, when a believer dies, his soul and spirit go straight to heaven. The paradise side of hades is currently and forever completely empty. (Luke 16:19–31; 2 Cor. 5:8; Eph. 4:8).

Hades, the holding place for those who rejected God and Christ, continues to increase in population. Hades is not purgatory; there is no such thing as purgatory. According to Hebrews 9:27, "It is appointed for man to die once and then the judgment." No intercessor or clergy can pray the souls out of hades, not on the first day, not on the fortieth day, not on any day. Tragically, the next "home" for those in hades is eternal hell, also known as the Lake of Fire (Rev. 20:10).

Where are hades and hell located? According to Jonah 2:2, hades is in the belly of the earth. And according to Ephesians 4:9–10, "Now this, He (Jesus) ascended— what does it mean but that He also first descended into the lower parts of the earth (hades)? He who descended is also the One who ascended far above all the heavens, that He might fill all things."

To further support the location of hades, David writes in Psalm 63:9, "But those (wicked) who seek my life to destroy it, shall go into the lower parts of the earth."

Jesus descended to hades in soul and spirit, not body. Hades is in the depths of the earth (Eph. 4:9), houses the ungodly after their death, and it is temporary. Hell, on the other hand, is in "outer darkness" and will house the ungodly for all eternity (Matt. 22:11–13). Hades, therefore, is the tormented transitional station preceding the place of unending torment, the Lake of Fire. Hell is not a concept. The reality of its existence holds "rewards or amenities" filled with eternal gnashing of teeth.

Who controls hades? Satan does not control hades, nor does he control hell! "Sheol (hades) is naked before Him (God) and destruction (death and hades) has no covering" according to Job 26:6, meaning God sees all and nothing escapes Him. Jesus said in Revelation 1:18, "I am He who lives, and was dead, and behold, I am alive forevermore. Amen. And I have the keys of hades and of death." Whoever holds the keys holds the power. Jesus alone!

Jesus spoke of hades in Luke 16:19–31. As we discussed, hades was divided into two regions; one, the side of torment, where the rich man's soul and spirit went after he died; and the other, the paradise side, where the poor man Lazarus' soul and spirit went after he died.

The rich man did not end up in the tormented side because he was rich; he ended up there because he ignored and scorned God. The poor man did not end up in paradise because he was poor; he ended up there because he honored and accepted God. There was a wide gulf in between the two sides and crossing over was impossible. The occupants in torment were further anguished as they witnessed the paradise side and yearned for water.

Today, if you were to peek into the pits of hades, you would see that they yearn for joy. Yearn for hope. Yearn for love. Yearn for goodness. Yearn for rest. They will never get water. They will never receive joy. They will never sense hope. They will know that they rejected God's love and will forever be separated from His presence. They will never have rest...for all of eternity.

Why did Jesus go to hades? On the day of His death, as His body lay in the tomb, Jesus descended to the paradise side of hades in soul and spirit and "led the captives captive" according to Ephesians 4:8; He took the souls and spirits of Abraham, Isaac, Jacob, Joseph, and all the God-fearing Old Testament saints to heaven, presenting them to the Father because of the blood He spilled on the cross. Why were they called "captives?" Though they were in a comfortable place, paradise, they were not yet in the third heaven in the presence of God. Why are they now "captive?" Currently, though their spirits and souls are in highest heaven, their human bodies remain on earth; they are "captive" in eternal bliss while their bodies are "captive" in the ground, awaiting to be glorified during the rapture, the imminent coming of the Lord to take believers up to heaven (1 Thess. 4:16).

Jesus also went to the tormented side of hades in soul and spirit on the day of His death according to 1 Peter 3:19–20 and "preached to the spirits in prison who formerly were disobedient." He alone is salvation. But did he really preach in hades? The word "preach" in the Greek in this context is *kerysso*. which means "to proclaim." Jesus proclaimed that He is alive; He is risen; He is victorious; He has overcome; He is God! Those on the tormented side heard Him preach, or proclaim victory over sin and death, but will never be able to receive salvation.

After one's last breath on earth, there are no more opportunities to come to Christ...unless, as we occasionally hear, that person is miraculously raised from the dead, comes back to the land of the living, and then accepts Him.

These "spirits in prison" saw the risen Savior! They saw the conquering Lord! They saw the King of kings and the Lord of lords! Jesus proclaimed to all the Old Testament souls and spirits who scorned His Father that

He Himself, as the Messiah and Savior, is God, and no death, no hell, no hades, no evil force, no demon, no Satan, no curse, no denial, no betrayal, no trial, no hatred, no cross and no death could keep Him down in the grave! He made a public spectacle of Satan and the demons and totally disarmed them (Col. 2:15). They all saw the One they had pierced. They all saw the One they had rejected. They all saw pure love. They all saw the One who offered them the greatest gift of eternal life. They all saw the only One who had granted them hope and joy, and it dawned on them: they, on their own accord, had rejected true life and embraced eternal death.

Those in hades wish they could call or text family members, telling them, "This place is for real! I'm stuck here in this miserable place...it's horrible...but hell is to come...and I hear that's eternal...I can't take this anymore...suffering every second...no relief...no help...no hope...no goodness...no light...no laughter...no friends... no family...no fellowship...no peace...no joy..how in the world am I gonna survive hell? I thought this place was a joke until I ended up here. I thought Jesus was a waste of time, until I saw His beauty. I thought demons were cartoon characters, until they dragged me to this godless pit! They are horrible creatures. They sting like scorpions. The physical pain is unspeakable. The mental torment is unbearable. The memories of the past are unforgettable. The reality of my existence is intolerable. Excruciating! Agonizing! Get me out! Get me out of here! These wretched demons torment me with their shrieking cries. They constantly terrify me, threaten me, and traumatize me! Please, I beg of you, listen to me. Get a Bible. Read it! Study it! Believe it! Christ is the real deal! He did die. He did suffer. But He is alive. And He's the real Savior! Please, please, listen to me...don't mock Christ...don't ignore Him...don't reject Him...believe in Him...call upon His name...go to Him...and don't end up in hell with me!"

Those in heaven wish they could call or text us as well, encouraging us, "This place is for real! Forgive those who hurt you! It's not worth carrying a grudge! Cancel their debts...you're not letting them off..you're letting yourself off and freeing yourself! Consider your trials as momentary...you won't even remember them up here! Don't get into stupid verbal fights! Get your Bible out. Read it. Devour it. Study it. Meditate on it. Love it. Listen to it. Follow it! They are not just words... they are your very life! Delight in the Lord! Desire Him! Talk to Him...He so longs to talks with you...He so longs to love you! Listen to Him...He will guide you, counsel you, direct you, and watch over you! He has chosen you! He has set you apart! My heart is bursting with joy! Oh my! The colors are so alive here! The music makes my heart explode with joy! The songs are so beautiful! The words...they are so new, so fresh, so heartwarming. I've never heard words like this before! I see God...I mean I really see Him...He is so stunning! His throne shines like diamonds. He is so lovely yet so majestic. Lightning and thunder proceed from His throne. An intense emerald rainbow surrounds Him! Angels bow down before Him...multitudes kneel before Him...we worship Him for He is so good. I walk with the Good Shepherd. His love is overwhelming me. His grace is uplifting me. His sacrifice on the cross saved me. Can't wait to see you here. Our God will see you through...He will make a way in your wilderness...and give you streams in your wasteland! He will make all things new! Am I really here? I thought this was a dream...but this is for real..yes, yes, it's for real...TGIH! TGIH! Thank God It's Heaven!"

1 1

Where in the World is Heaven?

In this chapter, we will explore the location of heaven and its significance for the believer as well as the unbeliever.

David prophesied in Psalm 16:10, "You (God) will not leave my soul in Sheol (hades) nor will You allow Your Holy One (Jesus) to see corruption." God would not allow His Son to stay in Sheol, nor would He allow His Son to see corruption in the grave! Jesus visited hades, but did not stay there, and He laid dead in the grave but rose on the third day.

David also prophesied in Psalm 68:18, "You (Christ) have ascended on high (to the third heaven); You have led captivity captive." According to Ephesians 4:9–10, "What does it mean (that Jesus ascended to heaven) but that He also first descended into the lower parts of the earth (before ascending to heaven in soul and spirit, He visited hades)? He who descended is also the One who ascended far above all the heavens, that He might fill all things (Jesus rules over all places)."

Right after His death, Jesus went to the paradise side of hades to take believers home to heaven. He also visited the tormented souls of hades to proclaim His victory over sin, evil, Satan, demons, and death. The Old Testament saints were considered "captives" because though they were in the paradise side of hades, they were not in the presence of God in heaven. As we read in chapter ten, when they were taken to heaven by Jesus, they became "captive," immersed in God's goodness and presence, and "shackled" by God's mercies and favor. Where is Christ now? He is in heaven at God's right hand where angels, authorities, and powers have been made subject to Him (1 Peter 3:22).

We know that hades is in the lower parts of the earth and hell is in outer darkness, but where exactly is heaven? There are three heavens that the Bible defines, and the fourth, when we consider eternity:

1. The first heaven is what we know as our immediate atmosphere where birds and airplanes fly. We read about this in Genesis 1:20 where on the

fifth day of creation God created the birds that
fly above the earth across the face of the firma-
ment of the heavens. We read in Jeremiah 4:25
that the "birds of the heavens had fled."

2. The second heaven is outer space (the sun, moon
   and stars). We read about this in Psalm 19:1–3
   (NIV84), "The heavens declare the glory of God,
   the skies proclaim the works of His hands. Day
   after day they pour forth speech. Night after
   night they display knowledge. There is no speech
   or language where their voice is not heard." It is
   also where Satan and his demons fight spiritual
   battles. In Daniel 10:12–14, Daniel was told that
   God (in the third heaven) answered his prayer the
   first day he prayed, but it was delayed by conflict
   (in the second heaven) for twenty-one days.

3. The third heaven is the house of God. We read
   about the third heaven in Isaiah 14:13–14 when
   Satan attempted to trump God by saying, "I (Satan) will also sit on the mount of the congrega-
   tion on the *farthest sides of the north*; I will ascend
   above the heights of the clouds; I will be like the
   Most High (God)." Heaven is not "up." It is located at the farthest north. In Job 37:22 we read, "He
   (God) comes from the north as golden splendor;

with God is awesome majesty." The apostle Paul was taken up to the third heaven and was in the glory of God (2 Cor. 12:2). The psalmist declared in Psalm 115:3, "Our God is in heaven; He does whatever He pleases."

Today's existing third heaven is not eternal and will pass away along with the earth (Matt 24:35; Rev. 21:1). Many people do not understand this notion, arguing, "Wait! How can you say that? Is God not synonymous with heaven? How then could He get rid of heaven?" At the present time, God's home is the third heaven, but He is not synonymous with heaven. He is synonymous with holiness. Heaven does not make Him God. Rather, God's presence makes His abiding place heaven.

4. There will be a future "fourth" heaven, our permanent and eternal home. This abode is now being "built" in the third heaven by the Great Carpenter and Creator, Jesus Christ. Just before His crucifixion, Jesus told his disciples, "Let not your heart be troubled; you believe in God, believe also in Me. In My Father's house (the third heaven) are many mansions; if it were not so, I would have told you. I go to prepare a place for

you (the fourth heaven). And if I go and prepare a place for you, I will come again and receive you to Myself (rapture of Christ followers); that where I am, there you may be also" (John 14:1–3). The fourth heaven will descend as the new heaven, the new Jerusalem, from the third heaven to the new earth (Rev. 21:9–27).

When will this transformation occur? If you were to study prophecy, you would recognize that the season of man's reign on earth is nearing its termination. The rapture is imminent when Christ will take believers to the third heaven in their glorified bodies.

"Behold, I (apostle Paul) tell you (believers) a mystery: We shall not all sleep (many believers will be caught up in the rapture without experiencing physical death), but shall all be changed (receive our glorified bodies, a new, young-looking, immortal body that is incapable of sinning, dying or becoming ill, yet not losing its characteristic facial features)—in a moment, in the twinkling of an eye, at the last trumpet. For the trumpet will sound, and the dead (believers' bodies whose souls and spirits are in the third heaven) will be raised incorruptible, and we shall be changed (receive immortal bodies). For this corruptible must put on incorruption, and this mortal must put on immortality" (1 Cor. 15:51–53).

A horrifying seven-year tribulation will ensue on earth after the rapture as unbelievers will face the most tragic and chaotic time in history. This will culminate in the battle of Armageddon, where Christ will wipe out all world powers in what is called His Second Coming. He will then reign for one thousand years on earth during the period known as the Millennium, a period filled with equity, peace, and justice. After the thousand years, the wicked of all time will then be judged at the Great White Throne and sentenced to hell. After this last judgment, eternity will begin as time comes to an end, with the climactic descent of the new heaven upon the new earth, the new abode for the redeemed.

We will study this subject further in chapter twenty-eight and get a glimpse of heaven on earth! The fourth heaven will be exciting! Filled with singing! Discovering! Exploring! Laughing! Living! Loving! Enjoying! Resting! Worshiping! Uncompromising! Unending!

To simplify the meaning of the different heavens, let us think of it in this manner:

1. The first heaven is what we can see and look at directly during the daytime. (We are unable to look at the sun directly; therefore, the sun is excluded).

2. The second heaven is what we can see at nighttime. (The second heaven includes the moon and stars as well as the sun which gives light to the moon).

3. The third heaven, the house of God, farthest north, is what we can see by faith.

4. The "fourth" heaven will be present on the new earth and will replace the intermediate and temporary third heaven. Believers will live in the presence of God for all of eternity.

What happens to our loved ones, believers in Christ, when they die? Their bodies may be placed in the ground or cremated. They may not even have died of a natural death, being killed in a war, mangled in an accident, or drowned at sea, never to be found. That's the physical being. A believer's physical body, though dead, is considered to be "sleeping" (1 Thess. 4:14) and will be glorified at the very moment of the rapture (1 Cor. 15:42–43). In the meantime, they have transitional bodies in the third heaven as they are "clothed with white robes" as spoken of the martyrs (Rev. 7:9).

After Jesus' resurrection, the soul and spirit of the ones who are born again, bought by the blood of the Lamb, go straight to the third heaven at the time of physical death. How do we know? According to 2 Cor. 5:8, to be absent from the body is to be present with the Lord. According to Philippians 1:23, for a believer, to depart or to die physically is to be with Christ. Believers who die today are redeemed and will not spend any time in the paradise side of hades as the Old Testament saints did; they will go straight into the presence of God! It brings immense joy to my heart when I think of my sweet dad who is now beholding the very God who created him and called him His own!

Conversely, the soul and spirit of the one who rejects Christ go to the torment side of hades at physical death. They will be kept there until the end of the Millennium, or the thousand-year reign of Christ on earth, at which time they will all meet their Maker at the Great White Throne. When one checks into hades, they can never check out except for their eternal entrance into hell.

Is it only the wicked that will end up in hades? No, surprisingly, there will be multitudes of decent and loving people who will end up in hades and will ultimately go to hell. There will be a lot of good people in hell: people who helped, who gave, who served, who were innovators, who built, who contributed; yet they dismissed their Creator and despised their Savior. They had no choice as to who their Creator was, but they did have a choice as to who their Savior would be, either trusting in themselves for their own salvation, or trusting in Christ and His finished work on the cross.

A Glimpse of Today's Heaven

What are Christ followers experiencing in heaven right now? Heaven today will not be the same as the heaven in eternity. I don't believe streets of gold exist in the present third heaven. These streets will exist in the fourth heaven, the new Jerusalem, the eternal and new heaven that will descend to the new earth after the Millennium (Rev. 21:21).

Two of Christ's twelve disciples, Paul and John, gave us a glimpse of the third heaven in their writings.

Paul tells us in 2 Corinthians 12:1–4 that he was caught up into paradise, the third heaven, and heard an "inexpressible word, it is not lawful for a man to utter." This one phrase gives us a hint of what heaven is like at this very moment. Brilliant colors that give light to the eyes. Melodies that soothe the heart. Worship that revives the soul. Indescribable words that finally speak of un-adulterated love. Joy that makes the feet dance. Hope that makes the face smile. Compassion that makes tears stop. Restoration that heals all illnesses. Forgive-ness that erases the past. Peace that makes the soul leap with joy, removing all fear, doubt, and worry. Oh, how beautiful! How wonderful! How breathtaking!

John, who was also taken up to the third heaven in the spirit, saw the throne room of God as it will appear dur-ing the tribulation period. He saw God, sitting on the throne, having the appearance of diamond-like (righ-teousness) and crimson-like (salvation) stones with an emerald-like rainbow around His throne. Around the throne were twenty-four elders (representing the church, the redeemed, the saved, the believers in Christ) clothed in white robes (purity) with crowns of gold on their heads (royal, children of the King). Lightning and thundering proceeded from the throne of God (sover-eignty and might of God).

Before the throne, John saw lamps depicting the pres-ence and character of the Holy Spirit. There was a sea of glass-like crystal before the throne of God. Four living creatures, cherubim, were around the throne, worship-ing God, proclaiming, "Holy, holy, holy, Lord God Al-mighty, who was and is and is to come!" The redeemed bow down before God and worship Him, saying, "You are worthy, O Lord, to receive glory and honor and power; for You created all things, and by You will they exist and were created." (Rev. 4:1–11).

Our God is worthy.
Our God is holy.
Our God is mighty.
Before Him is the glassy sea which depicts His purity.
Our God is surrounded by angels who rejoice in jubilee.
The redeemed worship Him wholeheartedly.
His anointed gather in a most blessed assembly.
Truly, truly...our God is altogether lovely!

In his vision, John waited to see the Lion of the tribe of Judah, Jesus Christ our Lord, but when he saw Him, he saw the Lamb as though He had been slain. Slain? In heaven? There will be no scars in heaven...with one exception. Jesus has risen. He is with the Father in heaven. He is perfect. He is God. He is the Word. According to Psalm 27:4, He is perfect in beauty. Yet, He retains His scars. Why? His wounds, His scars, His blood, His obedience unto death, and His resurrection are the reasons why believers have access, a "backstage pass" and admission into heaven. His scars will remain as a testimony and as an eternal reminder of our atonement and righteousness in and through Christ.

Revelation 5:1-14 reveals apostle John's vision, where Jesus took a scroll with seven seals from His Father's hand and was given the authority to open the seals to initiate the seven-year tribulation. All of heaven bowed down to worship Jesus. The redeemed joined with their harps and worshiped the Lamb of God. The saints sang, "You are worthy to take the scroll, and to open its seals; for You were slain and have redeemed us to God by Your blood out of every tribe and tongue and people and nation. And have made us kings and priests to our God; and we shall reign on the earth" (Rev. 5:9–10).

Every inhabitant in heaven sang, "Worthy is the Lamb who was slain to receive power and riches and wisdom and strength and honor and glory and blessing!" (Rev. 5:12).

Our Christ is worthy. Many leaders have exercised power to rule the earth, but man's heart is filled with greed, grudges, war, sin, and jealousy. Only Christ is able to rule in righteousness, in goodness, in mercy, in love, in truth, in peace, and in equity!

Note the different ethnic backgrounds in heaven, saints of every tongue, every tribe, every nation! We will not lose our identity, but we will not be the center of attention. The Lamb who was slain; the Lion who roars;

our Christ is the focal point, for by Him, not only were all things created that are in heaven and on earth, but all things exist through Him and for Him, and in Him all things consist! (Col. 1:16–17). No one will be saying, "Oh, look at him; look at her; he is black; she is white." Why? Because we are not going to heaven to worship ourselves. We are going to heaven to worship the Savior who was slain, the Lion who will eternally reign!

The blood of the Lamb, which gives us forgiveness and salvation, is the only means of entering into heaven. No money. No degree. No beauty. No competency. No sorcery. No army. No committee. No trickery. No new gods or gods of antiquity. Nothing that is earthly. Only the blood of Jesus. Only by the blood of the Lamb. Only by the blood of our Savior!

No one in their right frame of mind would call upon an ophthalmologist, neurologist, or gastroenterologist to treat an erratic heart rhythm; instead, one would call upon a cardiologist to find the cause of the condition, diagnose the problem, treat it, and prevent it from occurring again. No one in all of history can cure our spiritually erratic and tragic arrhythmia called sin except One. Make sure you go to the right doctor, the doctor of all doctors, the surgeon of all surgeons, the Great Physician, Jesus Christ!

Accept Jesus' invitation in Matthew 11:28–30, "Come to Me all who labor and are heavy laden, and I will give you rest. Take My yoke upon you and learn from Me, for I am gentle and lowly in heart, and you will find rest for your souls. For My yoke is easy and My burden is light." Heed His counsel in Revelation 22:12, "And behold, I am coming quickly, and My reward is with Me, to give to everyone according to his work."

Will you continue to ignore the chaotic rhythm in your spirit that desperately cries out for a Savior? Join instead those who are finally home with their Redeemer, singing, "Thank God for His tender mercies, thank God for His untainted love, thank God for His beloved Son's sacrifice, thank God for redeeming me out of destruction, and, yes, glory, glory, hallelujah. TGIH! Yes, yes, yes, Thank God It's Heaven!"

II. Heaven Tomorrow

From the Rapture through the Milennium

The Lost Ark of the Covenant

Many believe that the ark of the covenant was lost in 586 BC when King Nebuchadnezzar of Babylon attacked Jerusalem and carried off many of the articles of the temple. There is also a belief that the ark may be in Ethiopia. These assumptions, however, are not historically validated. What many don't know is that the actual ark is not lost.

When Moses was told to make the ark of the covenant, he made a copy of the actual ark which is in heaven; the real ark remains in heaven; the location of the ark made by Moses is unknown.

In Revelation 11:19, we read that when the seventh trumpet was sounded, "The temple of God was opened in heaven, and the ark of His covenant was seen in His temple." Yes, the third heaven houses the original temple and the original ark!

The high priests of Israel were in the order of Levi, and specifically, of the house of Aaron. The High Priest of heaven, Jesus Christ, is in the order of Melchizedek and of the house of God, who had no beginning or ending (Heb. 5:6; 7:3,17, 21). The high priest offered animal sacrifices; Jesus offered up Himself (Heb.7:27). According to Hebrews 8:1–2, Jesus Christ, the Great High Priest who is seated at the right hand of the throne of the Father in heaven, is the minister of the heavenly sanctuary and of the true tabernacle which the Lord erected without the hands of man. The heavenly sanctuary has a better mediator, a better promise, a better covenant, each saint with a spotless conscience, and an eternal inheritance because of the perfect sacrifice, Jesus Christ (Heb. 8:1–13;9:1–14).

What purpose would the temple as well as the articles of the temple, including the ark of the covenant, serve in the third heaven when we know that Jesus Christ is the true Mercy Seat? Everything in life. Everything in creation. Everything visible. Everything invisible. Everything in eternity. Everything on earth. Everything in heaven. All things. Point. To. Christ! He is the Bread of Life. He is the Light of the World. He is the perfect sacrifice. He is head of the temple. He is the Word. "For by Him all things were created that are in heaven and that are on earth, visible and invisible, whether thrones or dominions or principalities or powers. All things were created through Him and for Him. And He is before all things and in Him all things consist" (Col.1:16–17).

Even if people reject or ignore Him, the only reason they stand, breathe, and live is because He loves His creation! He does not wish that anyone should perish (2 Peter 3:9). He is giving you opportunity after opportunity to come to Him and live a life of abundant goodness and joy!

1 4

Ugly Times

What is the next event on the prophetic calendar and what will set off the seven-year tribulation? Are we just creatures who aimlessly live and die, or do we have hope for a better future, a heavenly future? The redeemed are filled with a blessed hope because the next major event in the prophetic timetable is the rapture, where Christ will come to take His Church, His beloved believers, home to be with Him. Not everyone who attends church will be raptured. Instead, raptured saints are those who love Christ, who have been bought by the blood of the Lamb, who honor Him, walk with Him, are committed to Him, and trust His Word. Faithful believers will be caught up in the air, *harpazo*, in the Greek.

We are currently in the Church Age, a time between the crucifixion and the rapture. The book of Revelation speaks of seven churches and we are in the period of the last church, the seventh church, Laodicea. This means that we are living in the last days. How do we know? Prophesies that seemed implausible in the past are dawning upon us...such as Russia, Turkey, and Iran becoming allies as was prophesied 2,500 years ago...to attack Israel in the Gog and Magog War. This unholy alliance is now ready with boots on the ground in Syria to engage in warfare with Israel! Other Arab nations will also join the coalition. For instance, Iran has infiltrated Lebanon with arms (Lebanon is noted as "Tyre" in Ps. 83:7), just north of Israel, and has made its plans plain to the world: obliterate the Jews (Ezekiel 38–39; Psalm 83).

Once the rapture occurs, Israel will sign a treaty with Arab nations, courtesy of the Antichrist. This treaty sets the seven-year tribulation in motion. Having the treaty signed, Israel will feel safe, and that is when the Gog and Magog Wars will occur. The Arab countries will attack Israel in its "safety" but will not succeed in annihilating God's chosen people; instead, those who attack will find themselves battling God, a futile cause! (Dan. 9:27; Ezek. 38:14; 39:1–4).

Daniel was told of the signs of last days, "But you, Daniel, shut up the words, and seal the book until the time of the end; many shall run to and fro and knowledge shall increase." Travel and knowledge have increased exponentially in our days...a telltale sign of the end times (Dan. 12:4)

The passage in 2 Timothy 3:1–5 also makes it clear, "But know this, that in the last days perilous times will come. For men will be lovers of themselves, lovers of money, boasters, proud, blasphemers, disobedient to parents, unthankful, unholy, unloving, unforgiving, slanderers, without self-control, brutal, despisers of good, traitors, head-strong, haughty, lovers of pleasure rather than lovers of God, having a form of godliness but denying its power. And from such people turn away!"

Does this not sound like the daily news?

Perilous times? Consider today's wars, famine, viruses, and disasters.

Lovers of themselves, lovers of money, boasters, proud, haughty? Consider today's entertainment.

Slanderers? Consider your neighbor; consider your friends; consider your family.

Unthankful? Consider ourselves.

Having a form of godliness but denying its power? Consider many of the churches in America!

What are the "vitals" of this church era? The church is neither cold nor hot, but it is lukewarm. It sees itself as rich, wealthy, and not needing anything, but according to Christ it is "wretched, miserable, poor, blind, and naked." (Rev. 3:17). It's actually in a spiritually erratic and tragic rhythm! What is causing it? Fear of man. Fear of critics. Fear of being shut down. Love of man's approval. Love of the world. Love of self.

Christ longs for His Church to be revived! He stands in its midst; He provides healing salve; He sends His Holy Spirit. Despite the pitiful condition of the church, He is still in its midst! (Rev. 1:13, 20).

Christ spoke of the rapture in John 14:1–4, "Let not your heart be troubled; you believe in God, believe also in Me. In My Father's house are many mansions; if it were not so, I would have told you. I go to prepare a place for you. And if I go and prepare a place for you, I will come again and receive you to Myself that where I am, there you may be also. And where I go you know, and the way you know."

Jesus tells us exactly what will happen:

1. At this time, the Great Carpenter, Jesus Christ, is preparing custom-built rooms for us! He is in the third heaven, building our abode which will be the "fourth" and eternal heaven for His children.

2. He is coming back in the rapture to receive us to Himself.

3. He is taking us to where He is, to the third heaven. God raised Christ from the dead and seated Him at His right hand in the heavenly places far above all principality, power, might, and dominion (Eph. 1:20–21). When the right time comes, Christ will come to take us home!

4. After we have spent seven years in the third heaven and one thousand years reigning on earth with Christ, then we will experience the "fourth" heaven. According to Revelation 21:2, the "fourth" and eternal heaven will descend to the new earth, where we will literally have "heaven on earth" for all eternity!

For those who don't know Christ...you still have time before the rapture. Grace is extended to you. God's arms are wide open to accept you. He is ready to run to you, pick you up and carry you. All you need to do is turn to Him! Come to Calvary's cross. Accept the Savior's divine blood of salvation, protection and healing! Turn away if you wish...you will never find what you are looking for, and even if you find it, by the time you get it, it will be outdated, and you will not be satisfied. Only Jesus can satisfy you because He is the only One who truly loves you!

For those who know Christ but are being choked by the thorns of this world...may I be frank with you? You need to turn off the all the clutter, the noise, and the madness. If you are watching and listening to everything the world listens to, why do you think you will get different results? You are running after everything except God. You are searching everywhere except God's Word. You are trusting everyone except Jesus Christ. You are using every resource except the Holy Spirit. It's time for you to stop the madness. It's time for you to stop the complaining. It's time for you to stop the vanity. It's time for you to get on your knees, repent, and seek God with all your heart. Then sit and rest in the Lord ... and watch the thorns in your life wither away as your soul begins to thrive!

I'll Meet You in the Air

What happens to believers as they are raptured? When my sweet father died and was buried, we placed his body in a coffin and then placed him in the ground. His body is still on earth, but his soul and spirit are in heaven. When the rapture occurs, his body will be glorified, changed in a one trillionth of a second, and it will unite with his glorified spirit and soul alongside Christ in the air to be taken to heaven. This will occur for all the redeemed who have died in Christ.

What happens to the redeemed if we are still on earth and are living when the rapture occurs? We too will be raptured, with our new glorified bodies and meet the Lord in the air. As you fly through the ceiling and the roof, don't sweat about getting a subdural hematoma (head bleed) and the nastiest headache of your life... because there will be no need for Excedrin in heaven and neurosurgeons will not have any of their gadgets to operate! Jesus walked through doors and walls in His glorified body, and we'll get to go through ceilings and roofs with ease and without injury!

Paul spoke of the rapture in 1 Corinthians 15:51–55, "Behold, I tell you a mystery. We shall not all sleep, but we shall all be changed—in a moment, in a twinkling of an eye, at the last trumpet. For the trumpet will sound, and the dead will be raised incorruptible, and we shall be changed. For this corruptible must put on incorruption, and this mortal must put on immortality. So when this corruptible has put on incorruption, and this mortal has put on immortality, then shall be brought to pass the saying that is written, 'Death is swallowed up in victory. O Death where is your sting? O Hades, where is your victory?'"

Paul calls the state of my dad's buried body in the grave as "sleeping." It means that his body will wake up on the glorious day of the rapture and be completely renewed, incorruptible, and immortal! Death will be conquered as hades has no hold on my father or any saint who has died in Christ. On the other hand, we who are living will be "changed," meaning our bodies will instantly become glorified, renewed, incorruptible, and immortal as we meet the Lord in the air. Our soul will also be glorified in that instant, and we shall be whole!

We find in Philippians 3:21 that a glorified body is a transformed body in the likeness of Christ, "For our citizenship is in heaven, from which we also eagerly wait for the Savior, the Lord Jesus Christ, who will transform our lowly body that it may be conformed to His glorious body, according to the working by which He is able even to subdue all things to Himself."

We find great hope in reading 1 Thessalonians 4:16–18, "For the Lord Himself will descend from heaven with a shout, with the voice of an archangel, and with the trumpet of God. And the dead in Christ will rise first. Then we who are alive and remain shall be caught up (*Harpazo* in the Greek) together with them in the clouds to meet the Lord in the air. And thus, we shall always be with the Lord. Therefore comfort one another with these words."

Only those who love Christ will hear His voice, the voice of an archangel and the trumpet of God! Those who are "sleeping" in Christ will rise first; we who are alive in Christ will rise next; we will all meet the Lord Jesus Christ in the air. And the beauty of the whole event is that from that moment on, we shall always be with the Lord!

What happens to the people who have died and rejected or ignored Christ? Their bodies will stay in the grave, and their spirits and souls will still remain imprisoned and tormented in hades until the Great White Throne Judgment. Paul spoke of their tragic end in 1 Corinthians 15:50, "Now this I say, brethren, that flesh and blood cannot inherit the kingdom of God; nor does corruption inherit incorruption."

And what of the people who are alive during the rapture and have no desire to know Christ? They will remain on earth and will face a hideous and merciless seven-year tribulation. However, they will have the opportunity to accept Christ and reject the 666-mark of the Beast.

You simply can't get eternal life without going through the One who offers it! But if you don't want Christ now, when you can turn on your air conditioner and lay on your comfortable couch, what will you do when fire rains from heaven and your skin is scorched by the sun during the tribulation?

Pre-Trib or Bust

Will we have to endure the tribulation spoken of in Revelation 6–19 or will we be spared? If you are bought by the blood of the Lamb, the quick answer is, "No, we will not have to endure the tribulation."

The Pre-Tribulation (Pre-Trib) view of future events states that the rapture is imminent, occurs just before the tribulation, and will include all the believers of the Church Age. This is a theologically sound viewpoint, and I am a strong proponent of it.

The Mid-Tribulation (Mid-Trib) view states that the rapture will occur after three-and-a-half years of the tribulation, and the children of God will have to endure three-and-a-half-years of the tribulation before they are raptured.

The Post-Tribulation (Post-Trib) view states that the rapture will occur after seven years of the tribulation, and the children of God will have to endure all seven years of the tribulation. The Mid-Trib and Post-Trib views are not consistent with God's character and the Word of God.

The word "church" is mentioned twenty times in the book of Revelation, nineteen times in the first three chapters and once in 22:16. The rapture occurs in chapter four, and believers enjoy the beauty, glory, and majesty of God in chapters four through five. The tribulation events are detailed from chapters 6–19, where the word "church" does not appear. Since the word "church" is not mentioned when the Bible speaks of the tribulation, it is not difficult to ascertain that the church is absent during the tribulation.

We read in Revelation 3:10 as the Lord speaks to the faithful church of Philadelphia, "Because you have kept My command to persevere, I also will keep you from the hour of trial which shall come upon the whole world, to test those who dwell on the earth." The Lord will keep His Church "from" the tribulation and not "through" the tribulation! The Lord also instructed us to watch and pray always that we may be counted worthy to escape all these things (tribulation) that will come to pass (Luke 21:36).

We read in 1 Thessalonians 1:10, "And to wait for Him from heaven, whom God raised from the dead, even Jesus who delivers us from the wrath to come." Many believe that Jesus will save us from hell but not the tribulation. In the context of the "Lord coming as a thief in the night," and not in the context of "hell," we read in 1 Thessalonians 5:9, "For God did not appoint us to wrath, but to obtain salvation through our Lord Jesus Christ, who died for us." The word "wrath" is orge in the Greek, and is the same word used for "wrath" (tribulation) in Revelation 6:16–17; 11:18; 14:9; 15:1,7; 16:18–19; 19:15.

In Titus 2:13, we are to be "Looking for the blessed hope and glorious appearing (rapture) of our great God and Savior Jesus Christ." In the Pre-Trib view, we are looking for the coming of Christ. In the Mid and Post-Trib views, people are looking for and trying to identify the Antichrist. In the Pre-Trib view, we are listening for the trumpet of the Lord. In the Mid- and Post- Trib views, people are listening for trouble.

If we summarize 1 Thessalonians 4:16–18, we will find:
1. Christ's shout, the voice of an archangel, and the trumpet of God coincide with Christ descending from heaven during the rapture.
2. The buried bodies of Christ followers will become glorified first and rise to meet Christ in the air.

3. The bodies of Christ followers who are still alive will then become glorified, meeting the Lord in the air.

4. We will then be with the Lord.

5. Christ followers who are currently on earth are to comfort one another with these words.

How would it sound to you if I were to tell you that you are going to go through hell on earth, be exposed to sun-scorching heat, hail, hunger, droughts, darkness, demons, famine, the 666-mark, the malicious and wicked Antichrist, having the grand reward of being beheaded...and yes...I'm pleased to be able to comfort you with these words! That is nonsense! We are faced with earthly tribulations, hardships in our homes, troubles in our work, and challenges in our daily lives, but we will not be facing God's divine wrath during the seven-year tribulation. Hallelujah to the Lamb of God!

Finally, there are sadly many victims of domestic violence who are scarred for life. I believe you would agree with me if I were to tell you that God is against domestic violence. Jesus' church is His bride (Rev. 19:7). Why would anyone think that He would allow us, His bride, to undergo domestic violence and face the tribulation? The ungodly and unbelievers are the object of God's wrath; not His Church; not Christ's bride! Jesus loves

His bride. He gave His life for His bride. He was slain for His bride. He will not beat up His bride. He will always bring honor to His bride! What a blessing and honor to be called the Bride of Christ, a title designated to all those who have accepted Him as their Lord and Savior! Always remember: you are greatly beloved by Christ.

1 7

Seven-Up or
Seven-Down

While believers will be in heaven after the rapture, what will happen to the unbelievers left behind on earth? They will be facing a seven-year tribulation, a hell-on-earth experience that you would definitely want to miss! If you are hesitating to accept Christ today, you will face cataclysmic events during the tribulation that will overwhelm you with fear and dread. Fear can cause people to make bad decisions. Today is the day of your salvation! While you have breath. While you have your sanity. While you are living in the comfort of your residence. While you are not threatened to bow to the Antichrist. Today...today...today is your day to accept Christ! (Heb. 3:7, 15; 4:7).

If believers don't yet attain or enjoy the eternal mansions spoken of in John 14:1–3 just after the rapture, what will we be doing in the third heaven and how long will we stay there? There will be many joys in heaven in a short seven-year span, three of which are the following:

1. Bema Seat, the judgment seat of Christ, believers receive rewards: (2 Cor. 5:10).

2. Marriage of the Lamb, believers are betrothed to Christ (Rev. 19:7).

3. Marriage supper of the Lamb, believers feast with Christ (Rev. 19:9).

In the meantime, what are the "rewards" of the tribulation on earth?

1. The Unholy Trinity: Satan, the Antichrist or the First Beast, and the False Prophet or the Second Beast terrorize earth dwellers during the seven-year tribulation (Rev. 6–19).

2. The seven seal judgments, the seven trumpet judgments; the seven bowl judgments will ravage the earth and its dwellers (Rev. 6–19).

3. The collapse of a one-world religion and one-world government will occur suddenly and swiftly (Rev. 17–18).

Where will you be spending the seven years after the rapture? "Seven-Up" with the beauty of the Lord or "Seven-Down" coming face to face with the Antichrist's wicked schemes? Can you confidently say that you will be in heaven, communing with our Lord? I pray that you can! The above-mentioned events are described in the following chapters and are thoroughly discussed in volumes one and two of my book, *Rev It Up—Verse by Verse*.

Heaven Bound

After the rapture, Christ followers will be in the third heaven for seven glorious years! This is what we've been anticipating! Let's dive in and explore what joys await us.

We will first undergo a judgment and a rewards ceremony. This is not a judgment that determines our final abode as in heaven or hell...we're already in heaven and will remain with the Lord forever! This event is what the Bible calls the "Bema Seat," where "we must all appear before the judgment seat of Christ that each one may receive the things done in the body, according to what he has done, whether good or bad" (2 Cor. 5:10).

If we dig further, we will find in 1 Corinthians 3:12–15, "Now if anyone builds on this foundation (Jesus Christ) with gold, silver, precious stones, wood, hay, straw, each one's work will become clear; for the Day (judgment day for Christ followers only) will declare it, because it will be revealed by fire; and the fire will test each one's work of what sort it is. If anyone's work which he has built on it endures, he will receive a reward. If anyone's work is burned, he will suffer loss; but he himself will be saved, yet so as through fire."

The believers' service will be "weighed" in attitude and in motive! According to Proverbs 16:2, "All the ways of a man are pure in his own eyes, but the Lord weighs the spirits." What is left after the fire will determine our privileges we have in heaven and for all of eternity!

It all sounds scary, but it is simply a reminder for us to redeem our time wisely while we live on earth (Eph. 5:16). We are saved by grace through faith...we did not deserve it, nor did we do anything to earn it or work for it (Eph. 2:8). Even "our" faith is given to us by God! (Rom. 12:3b). Once we are saved, our priorities change and we long to serve our Lord. Serving God does not save us; we serve God because we are saved.

Our years on earth are crucial. What we do for Christ after salvation will be rewarded and will translate into gifts, crowns, and positions in eternity. What we do in our own strength, in our own name, and for our own glory will be burned in the fire as wood, hay, and straw. Those in heaven will be rewarded according to their deeds just as those who will be going to hell will be "re-warded" for their works (Rom. 2:6). Jesus said, "And be-hold, I am coming quickly, and My reward is with Me, to give to everyone according to his work" (Rev. 22:12).

Everything we see will pass away. Leaders will die. Fol-lowers will fade. Fads will cease. The future does not belong to communism. The future does not belong to capitalism. The future belongs to Christ! Let us not jeopardize our rewards! Let us pursue the heart of God. Let us run the race, the few years given to us, looking unto Christ, the Author and Finisher of our faith! (Heb. 12:2).

1 9

Looking Fine!

What will we wear in heaven? We read in Revelation 4:4, "Around the throne were twenty-four thrones, and on the thrones, I saw twenty-four elders sitting, clothed in white robes, and they had crowns of gold on their heads." The elders represent believers of all times. We will be clothed in white because the spirit, soul and body will collectively and finally be purified. We will wear crowns of gold because we will reign with our Christ, having the title "royal priesthood" given to us by our Father (1 Peter 2:9).

When we are in Christ, our spirit becomes completely purified while we are still on earth. 2 Corinthians 5:17 supports this, "If anyone is in Christ, he is a new creation; the old has passed and the new has come." This view is also supported by 2 Corinthians 5:21, "He (Jesus Christ) who had no sin became sin (on the cross) so that we may become the righteousness of God in Christ."

I know a lot of Christ followers, including myself, who have strong intentions to live holy lives. However, frequently we don't look, speak or act like a new creation on any given day! Our old ways still tend to sneak up on us. Though our old nature is completely dead, its corpse, or learned behaviors, are still present. So how are we a "new creation"? Our spirit becomes renewed and sealed by the Holy Spirit when we accept Jesus Christ as our Savior and Lord and is the part of us that is fully redeemed. It does not need to mature or become pure...our spirit is holy in Christ!

1 John 3:9 states, "Whoever has been born of God does not sin, for His (Christ's) seed remains in him; and he cannot sin, because he has been born of God." How can this be? All Christ followers know that they sin! We sin in our mind and in our bodies, but we cannot sin in our spirit. In Christ, our spirit is holy, and nothing, not at any time, nor anyone in any given circumstance is able to taint it! Therefore, for Christ followers on earth, our salvation is one-third wholly and completely perfected!

Though Christ died for all three entities, the spirit, the soul (mind) and the body, the soul and body await their renewal. However, the saints who have gone before us to heaven have a spirit and soul that is completely sealed and wait for their glorified bodies which will occur during the rapture. For the saints, the believers, here on earth, we have a spirit that is completely sealed and wait for our renewed souls and glorified bodies which will occur during the rapture.

If we could only get our soul, our mind, to follow the spirit...oh, how glorious and joyful our stay on earth would be...and that is what we are urged to do in Romans 12:1–2...to transform our minds (souls) through the Word of God! By transforming our minds, we can experience the joys of heaven here and now!

Once we are raptured and enter heaven, our attempts to transform our minds will be pointless because all three, the body, soul and spirit will be one in Christ! We will finally be whole, unmarred and unblemished, permanently, completely and eternally! "Looking fine!" Yes! Yes! There is hope for us yet! "For now (in our earthly bodies), we see through a glass, dimly, but then (in heaven with our gloried bodies and souls) face to face. Now I know in part, but then I shall know just as I also am known" (1 Cor. 13:12).

2 0

No Homelessness

John wrote in Revelation 7:9–12 that he looked and, "Behold a great multitude which no one could number, of all nations, tribes, peoples, and tongues, standing before the throne and before the Lamb, clothed with white robes, with palm branches in their hands, and crying out with a loud voice saying, 'Salvation belongs to our God who sits on the throne and to the Lamb!' All the angels stood around the throne and the elders (church) and the four living creatures and fell on their faces before the throne and worshiped God, saying 'Amen! Blessing and glory and wisdom, thanksgiving and honor and power and might, be to our God forever and ever. Amen!'"

We continue to read in Revelation 7:15–17, "Therefore, they are before the throne of God, and serve Him day and night in His temple. And He who sits on the throne will dwell among them. They shall neither hunger anymore nor thirst anymore; the sun shall not strike them, nor any heat; for the Lamb who is in the midst of the throne will shepherd them and lead them to living fountains of waters. And God will wipe away every tear from their eyes."

Who are these innumerable people from "all nations, tribes, peoples, and tongues," standing before the throne, worshiping, serving, and receiving God's goodness? These are the martyrs who will die physically during the great tribulation, the last three-and-a-half years of the seven-year tribulation. And their spirits and souls join the redeemed who have been raptured. What a transition for them! From tragedy to victory! From dishonor to honor! From corruptible to incorruptible! From mortal to immortal! From being martyred by the Antichrist to being loved by Jesus Christ!

People love parties. People love celebrations. People love to be part of a family. People love to have someone they adore. Heaven will welcome those bought by the blood of the Lamb from every tongue and nation with open arms. There is no confusion such as was seen in Genesis 11 at the Tower of Babel, where everyone spoke a different language, chaos reigned, and the people were scattered all over the face of the earth. In heaven, there is harmony. There is serenity. There is purity. There is life for all eternity!

Do you ever wonder why there will be harmony without hostility, serenity without jealousy, and purity without bigotry in heaven? Why will we not be pointing fingers, slaying another with our tongues, or demeaning someone for their sex, creed, color, or background? As we discussed in chapter twelve, you and I are not the center of attention! Jesus Christ, the Lord of lords, the Lamb slain, the Lion resurrected, and God eternal...He is the essence of our existence and the foundation of our eternity!

Heaven is where the lonely become honored members of God's family. The humble will inherit God's goodness. And the redeemed live in the glory of God's righteousness. Psalm 68:6 will spring up to its full measure where "God will set the lonely in families!"

Loss of loved ones. Loss of hope. Loss of mind. Loss of worth. Loss of assets. Loss of dignity. Loss of breath. Loss of life. None of these will ever be experienced in heaven! There will never be hunger, homelessness, discomfort, thirst, illnesses, tears, theft, nor death. Even when we have been there ten thousand years or beyond ten billion years, all things will remain new, good, happy, and peaceful. In God's presence there will be fullness of joy! At God's right hand, there will be pleasures forevermore (Ps. 16:11)! At last! Safe at home in the arms of our loving Father!

2 1

For Richer, For Poorer

After receiving our just rewards at the Bema Seat, we, the redeemed, will be married to Christ. "Let us be glad and rejoice and give Him (God) glory, for the marriage of the Lamb has come, and His wife (His Church, true believers, Christ followers) has made herself ready. And to her it was granted to be arrayed in fine linen, clean and bright, for the fine linen is the righteous acts of the saints" (Rev. 19:7–8).

There will be no fleeting vows that we hear so often on earth, "I, such and such, take thee, such and such, to have and to hold from this day forward, for better, for worse, for richer, for poorer, in sickness and in health, to love and to cherish, until death do us part." The marriage in heaven will be an unbreakable, incorruptible, and an inseparable bond.

Since there will be no tragedies in heaven, the pledge will never be "for worse." Since there will be no poverty in heaven, the relationship will never be "for poorer." Since there is no disease in heaven, the union will never be "in sickness." Since there will be no death in heaven, the marriage will never be "until death do us part."

Can you hear the beauty of our future vow in your soul? "I, Jesus Christ, The Son of God, take thee, My loving bride, My Church, to be My beloved, to protect and treasure, from this day forward, for better, for richer, in perfect health, to love and to cherish from now throughout all of eternity."

There will be no fighting, no bickering, no belittling, no backstabbing, no head butting, no misunderstanding, no disputing, no quarreling, no squabbling, no clashing, no contesting, no separating, and no divorcing! Oh, happy and glorious day! TGIH! Thank God It's Heaven!

2 2

Cheers!

Then comes the supper of the Lamb! "Blessed are those who are called to the marriage supper of the Lamb!" (Rev. 19:9). Eat! Eat to your heart's content! There will be no cardiologist telling you to watch your cholesterol, walk 10,000 steps a day, don't sit on the couch, eat more vegetables, cut down on your ice cream, bread, cheese, and soda pops! No one will check your waist size, telling you to have a forty-inch or below waist size if you are a male and thirty-five-inch or below waist size if you are a female! No one will weigh you! No one will check your body mass index, BMI, telling the "patients" in heaven that they are overweight or obese! Eat! Eat to your heart's content! Be joyful! Be merry! Rejoice! Relish in the heavenly culinary delights, and rest in the beauty of Jesus Christ!

Our taste buds will explode. Sweet and sour will have been forgotten. New flavors. New tastes. New food.

New delicacies. It would be sensory overload here on earth...but just right...actually, perfect, in heaven!

We eat on earth to sustain life. But not in the third heaven. There, we will eat to enjoy fellowship and celebrate life together with our heavenly Father! How would you like that? Medium rare? Well done? It does not matter. Nothing is too hot. Nothing is too cold. Nothing is underdone. Nothing is overdone. The chef did not go to culinary school. He is not an "iron chef." This is the cuisine of Christ. It's mouthwatering, palate pleasing, heavenly tasting, heart pounding, jubilee dancing, no burden carrying, and the party is on and happening! Boring? No way! These are just the appetizers... the main course is called eternity with Christ! You will not be saying, "TGIF, Thank God it's Friday;" you will be hitting the dance floor, spinning, twirling, and singing, "TGIH! Thank God It's Heaven!"

Will You Take the 666?

It may surprise you that in His recorded words, Jesus spoke more about hell than He did about heaven. As you read the book of Revelation, you'll also find that two-thirds of the book, fourteen out of twenty-two chapters, focus on the tribulation and only two chapters address the new heaven.

When the rapture occurs, the world will immediately be in a state of chaos. Millions upon millions of Christ followers will be missing, having been taken up to the third heaven. There will be influential religious leaders who will convince their followers on earth that the event that just occurred could not be the rapture because they, as "godly" spiritual leaders, were not taken up. The newscasters will proclaim that UFOs snatched the "intolerant Christ-following bigots," and earth is so much better for it! While we enjoy the seven years of marriage

and feasting in heaven, earth dwellers will be stagger-
ing in torment and longing for a gateway of escape.

The seven seals of judgment will be opened by Christ
consecutively during the first three-and-a-half years of
the tribulation as God's throne of grace turns into God's
throne of wrath:

1. According to Revelation 6:1–2, the first seal will
   release the Antichrist riding on a white horse to
   bring "peace" into a world reeling in anarchy and
   mass confusion. Once the Antichrist fools the
   masses that he is the "savior" of the world, the
   second seal is opened.

2. According to Revelation 6:3–4, the second seal releases a red horse with its rider ushering in war.
   This correlates with Ezekiel 38–39, the Gog and
   Magog War, where Russia, along with Iran, Turkey, Somalia, and Libya will attack Israel. This
   aligns with Psalm 83:6 where Turkey, Saudi Ara-
   bia, Syria, Gaza, and Lebanon will unite to wipe
   Israel off the map. All these nations will tragically realize that they are not fighting against Israel but they are fighting against God, and five-
   sixths, or 83 percent, of the alliance population
   will be destroyed (Ezek. 39:2).

Even at the start of the twenty-first century, critics laughed at the thought of such an alliance between these nations. Let the mockers mock. Let
the scorners scorn. Let the hecklers heckle. Let
the taunters taunt! Russia, Turkey and Iran, the
unholy alliance, have already set foot in Syria,
just north of Israel, and are ready militarily to
attack Israel!

3. According to Revelation 6:5–6, the third seal
    releases a black horse with its rider ushering
    in famine. It's never wise to follow Satan. He is
    a liar, a thief, a master deceiver and will steal
    one's peace, one's joy, and one's life. How decep-
    tive! "Come, and taste of my goodness," he en-
    tices. "Taste my peace," he boasts, "Yes, taste my
    freedom, drink until you are satisfied, energize
    yourself with stimulating drugs; you deserve to
    be happy...so do what you want...life is a thrill...
    you only live once...who cares about others...
    live it up!" Once he lures you in, he beats you up
    with condemnation, plagues you with illnesses,
    blames it on God, and spits you out to die!

4. According to Revelation 6:7–8, the fourth seal
    releases a pale horse that will cause death upon
    earth's inhabitants, killing one-fourth of the

world's population. That's twenty-five percent! If the earth's population were ten billion during the tribulation, then two-and-a-half billion people will die in a very short segment of time!

5. According to Revelation 6:9–11, the fifth seal is opened and reveals heaven's countless martyrs who died for the sake of Christ. They are comforted by Christ, being assured that the Day of Vengeance (Second Coming of Christ at the end of the tribulation) is near.

6. According to Revelation 6:12–17, the sixth seal releases cosmic havoc, triggering the sun to darken, the moon to run bloody red, and the earth to quake. Mankind will continue to snub God in unbelief in their state of torment; they will ultimately, yet tragically too late, come to terms with the fact that there is no hope, no joy, and no eternal life apart from Christ.

7. According to Revelation 8:1–6, the seventh seal will release the seven trumpet judgments. Greater chaos awaits those who did not die during the six seals.

There will be such debris, such devastation, such disturbances, such disasters, such disorganization, such disillusionments, and such distress that Satan will grasp the slight hope left in peoples' hearts and splatter it on the scorched ground. No one will be able to give you liberty, but Satan will be happy to serve you with death.

The seven trumpets, released by the seventh seal, amplify the judgments that have already been poured out upon man (Revelation 8–9). How could so much wrath proceed from the throne of a loving God? According to 2 Peter 3:9, "The Lord is not slack concerning His promise as some count slackness but is longsuffering toward us not willing that any should perish but that all should come to repentance." He has "delayed" His coming so mankind would turn to Him and repent. Man creates the problems we face and the troubles that ensue. God has the answer, the one and only answer, the love of Jesus Christ. Because man refuses Christ's love, rejects His presence, and reviles His counsel, man will have to face God's wrath as He unleashes the seven trumpet judgments, carefully detailed in my book, volume one and two of *Rev It Up—Verse by Verse*.

By the end of the sixth trumpet judgment, half of the world's population will have died, and the seventh trumpet will issue the seven bowl judgments in the second half of the tribulation, in the last three-and-a-half years (Revelation 15–16). If the earth's population were ten billion at the time of the rapture, only five billion will be left alive after the sixth trumpet sounds. We are not talking "t" as in thousands or "m" as in millions. We are talking about "b" as in billions!

The 666-mark of the Antichrist will be implemented by the False Prophet in the second half of the tribulation known as the great tribulation. As the Holy Spirit leads us to Christ, the False Prophet will lead multitudes to the Antichrist. Without the 666-mark, no one will be able to buy or sell. Toilet paper and water bottles were difficult to come by during the Coronavirus pandemic; hardships will intensify in the great tribulation, when it will be impossible to buy anything without the 666-mark.

When you walk into a hospital or into my cardiology office, we will check your temperature by measuring the heat that dissipates from your forehead; this practice is conditioning people's mind for what is to come in the future, where a 666 chip in the forehead or right hand will be placed into people during the great tribulation. Many who are left behind will accept the 666-mark and will be "scanned" when they purchase a loaf of bread. They may get a bite to eat, but because they sold their soul to Satan by accepting the mark, they will forever be damned in hell and will be declared irredeemable (Rev. 13:8).

Once the last judgments, the bowl judgments, are poured out upon the godless, the end of this earth as we know it will draw ever so near as Jesus will come back (the Second Coming of Christ) to rid the earth of secular governments (Revelation 16–19).

So then, what is the "good news" about the seven-year tribulation? Millions upon millions will reject the 666-mark and turn to Christ! (Rev. 7:9–17). At the end of the tribulation, the existing earth dwellers will witness the collapse of all world governments, and the thousand-year reign of Christ on earth will begin! (Revelation 17–19).

Evil will be placed on hold and wars will cease during the Millennium. "He (Christ) shall judge between the nations and rebuke many people; they shall beat their swords into plowshares, and their spears into pruning hooks; nation shall not lift up sword against nation, neither shall they learn war anymore" (Isa. 2:4). Earth will be renovated, animals will become docile, and nations will seek the Lord (Isa. 11:6–16).

Unrighteousness, greed and bribes will halt during the Millennium. The Word of the Lord will go forth and will not return void. Justice will reign and will not be scorned or adulterated. Truth will flourish and will not succumb to lies because Satan will be bound during the thousand years. Equity shall reign and will not be subject to corrupt politics! Why? Because the Lord Jesus Christ, the Way, the Truth, and the Life, will rule. Come, Lord Jesus, come! (Ps. 96:10–13).

2 4

Zap that Nasty Rhythm

The elation escalates from the grandstands of heaven as we also witness the fall of all the earthly kingdoms. We'll be shouting, "Hallelujah! Salvation and glory and honor and power belong to the Lord our God!" (Rev. 19:1). The third heaven will then open and Christ, the faithful and true, whose eyes are like a flame of fire, will come to earth riding on a white horse. He will be wearing many crowns depicting Him as the supreme ruler of all the universe. And we, the redeemed, His Bride, will follow Him in His Second Coming on white horses as the campaign of Armageddon unfolds at the tail end of the seven-year tribulation.

"Now I saw heaven opened, and behold, a white horse. And He who sat on him was called Faithful and True, and in righteousness He judges and makes war. His eyes were like a flame of fire, and on His head were many crowns. He had a name written that no one knew except Himself. He was clothed with a robe dipped in blood and His name is called the Word of God. And the armies in heaven, clothed in fine linen, white and clean, followed Him on white horses. Now out of His mouth goes a sharp sword, that with it He should strike the nations. And He Himself will rule them with a rod of iron. He Himself treads the winepress of the fierceness and wrath of Almighty God. And He has on His robe and on His thigh a name written: King of kings and Lord of lords" (Rev. 19:11–16).

His eyes will penetrate every heart. His Word will dismantle every weapon. His righteousness will rule every nation. From the rising of the sun to the place where it sets, there is no other god, He is the Lord and there is none besides Him (Isa. 45:6).

Come all you kings of the earth. Come and draw your weapons. Bring your best battalions. Bring your finest warriors. Bring your mightiest soldiers. Fly your jets. Display your weapons of mass destruction. Activate your nuclear arms. Flex your muscles. Spread your lies. Laugh. Mock. Scorn. You will be dismantled by the Word of God, Jesus Christ, in one trillionth of a second! From dust you came, and to dust you will return, into oblivion, and then, into eternal hell.

All world powers, led by the armies of the East (with China in the lead) will come to fight in hopes of destroying Israel (Rev.16:12; Zech. 14:2); God will laugh at all the armies of the world, save the remnant of Israel, which He will have sheltered in Jordan during the great tribulation, and obliterate all world powers (Micah 2:12; Ps. 2:1–12). He will cast the Antichrist and the False Prophet into the Lake of Fire (Rev. 19:20). Open up hell's gates! Hell will gladly accept its very first occupants, the Antichrist and the False Prophet. Satan will not be cast into hell just yet; he will be bound and cast into the bottomless pit for one thousand years (Rev. 20:1–3). Whenever Satan is on the loose, there is war. Whenever he is bound, there is peace.

Currently, our world is in turmoil. Viruses spread rapidly. Wars declare instability. Resources wane unpredictably. People hurt each other increasingly. Hearts grow cold incessantly. One goes about his day anxiously. Countless walk about aimlessly. Children are brought up faithlessly. Many have chosen to live lawlessly. Television teaches immorality. Entertainment numbs the mind senselessly. People treat each other heartlessly. A one-world government is growing globally. God's goodness is snubbed tragically. Masses have rejected the gift of the Almighty. What in the world has happened to our humanity?

Our current situation, however, is nothing compared to what the earth will endure during the tribulation: utter chaos. The earth's "heartbeat" will be in atrial fibrillation: erratic, tragic, out of control, as was my patient's. What is the cause? Is it inequality, injustice, or bigotry? No! The cause of the man's problems is summed up in one word: sin. What is the cure? A peace treaty? A one-world government? Religion? The Antichrist? Money? More education? Social justice? More legislation? More reparations? More twelve-step programs? No! The only answer is Jesus Christ! He will return to "zap" the destructive rhythm of this earth, restoring it back to full health, where we will finally experience peace on earth and good will towards mankind!

Dashed to Pieces

According to Psalm 2, "let the nations rage against God!" Let the kings of the world plot against Christ, the Anointed One. Christ will return to earth after the seven-year tribulation and His feet will touch the Mount of Olives as He wars against all the nations who have come to destroy Jerusalem (Zech. 14:2–4). This war, the campaign of Armageddon, will stretch from Megiddo to Jerusalem to Petra, Jordan. These ominous events occur during the Second Coming of Christ; the First Coming culminated in His death on the cross, but the Second Coming will bring death to the wicked.

Christ will break all nations with a rod of iron and dash them to pieces like a potter's vessel. The campaign of Armageddon will bring all world powers and the one-world government that ruled during the tribulation to a screeching halt. Christ the Rock will shatter the gold, silver, bronze, iron, and clay figure, a symbol of dominant world powers, as prophesied in King Nebuchad-

SAMUEL A. KOLOGLANIAN, MD, FACC

nezzar's dream (Dan. 2:44). Our Redeemer, our Savior, our Creator lives, and in the end, He shall stand! All will bow. Christ shall stand! (Job 19:25).

The purpose of the tribulation is not only to punish the wicked, both Jews and Gentiles, and bring the one-world government to its knees, but also to save the Jewish remnant, which will be one-third of the entire Jewish population; the remnant will have been kept safe during the second half of the tribulation in Bozrah-Petra, Jordan (Isa. 34:6; Isa. 63:1; Zech. 13:8; Rev. 12:13–17). The Jewish remnant will look upon the One they have pierced, Jesus Christ, and will turn their hearts to Him as He saves them from the wretched hands of Satan at the end of the tribulation (Zech. 12:10).

We will then witness the judgment of the sheep and goats as noted in Matthew 25:31–46. By some miracle, there will be a score of people who will manage to survive the seven-year tribulation, the campaign of Armageddon and accept Christ as their Savior. They will be designated as "sheep" for they not only turned to Christ, but they protected their Jewish brethren, the Jewish remnant. They will hear the sweet words of Jesus, "Assuredly, I say to you, inasmuch as you did it (feeding the hungry, giving water to the thirsty, taking in the stranger, clothing the naked, caring for the sick, visiting the prisoner) to one of the least of these My brethren, you did it to Me" (Matt. 25:40). They will enter the Millennium without receiving their glorified bodies.

On the other hand, a considerable amount of people who manage to survive the seven-year tribulation and the campaign of Armageddon, but do not accept Christ, will be designated as "goats" and will be sent to hades to ultimately and eternally die in hell (Matt. 25:31–46). They will hear the heart-wrenching words of Jesus, "Assuredly, I say to you, inasmuch as you did not do it to one of the least of these, you did not do it to Me" (Matt. 25:45). They will be sent to hades for one thousand years till they meet their Maker once again to receive their final sentence at the Great White Throne Judgment of Christ (Rev. 20:11–15).

Live Long.
Live Strong.

While all unbelievers will face torment in hades and then ultimate hell, all believers will enter the Millennium, the earthly 1,000-year reign of Christ from Jerusalem. We will no longer be living in the third heaven. The earth will be completely renovated by God since it was completely devastated during the tribulation.

The Millennium Era is a literal period! Christ will rule with righteousness (Isa. 1:25–28; 11:3–5); there will be no wars (Isa. 2:4); wild and dangerous animals such as lions and snakes will do no harm (Isa. 11:6–8; 65:25); there will be no other governments (Isa. 11:1–2; 16:5); the human body will change where the blind shall see and the deaf shall hear (Isa. 32:3; 35:5–6); the wilderness will change where roses blossom in the desert (Isa. 32:15; 35:1, 6–7); joy and gladness will reside in our hearts (Isa. 35:10; 51:11); longevity will change where a 100-year old will be considered only a child (Isa. 65:20); work will change where people will enjoy the labor of their hands (Isa. 65:21–23); worship will change, where people will come to Jerusalem from all over the world to see and bow before Christ (Isa. 2:3).

Look no further for the fountain of youth. You will be living in the era of righteousness and wellness! Don't reach for the collagen or laser that will smooth out your face. Let go of the medicine cabinet. Stop adding doctor's names in your black book. Cast worry aside. Have no fear whether your vote will count or not. No insurance needed. The stock market will not exist. Your retirement is taken care of. No fear of abduction, sex trafficking, or rape. Sit down and take a break. Lay down and take a nap. Rise up and walk in peace. How wonderful! How beautiful! Everything you have ever pursued and longed for is found only in Jesus. Jesus alone!

The bodies of the tribulation martyrs will be raptured, or glorified, at the start of the Millennium as they too will reign with the saints who were raptured just before the tribulation. (Rev. 20:4–6). Those who were raptured are considered to have taken part in the "First Resurrection" and will never face the "Second Death," or eternal hell, which is kept for those who rejected Christ.

Those of us who were raptured just before the tribulation will have our glorified bodies and we, the Bride of Christ, will reign with Christ. The level and range of our reign will depend on the rewards we received during the Bema Seat Judgment as noted in chapter 18. We can neither sin, procreate, become ill, nor die in our new bodies.

The "sheep" who made it through the tribulation as well as the Jewish remnant will enter the Millennium without their glorified bodies and will be able to live up to one thousand years and procreate, repopulating the earth. How can their aging, or more accurately, the lack thereof, be possible? According to Ezekiel 47:12, there will be a river that will flow from God's Millennial temple built in Jerusalem, "Along the bank of the river, on this side and that, will grow all kinds of trees used for food; their leaves will not wither, and their fruit will not fail. They will bear fruit every month, because their water flows from the sanctuary. Their fruit will be for food, and their leaves for medicine." The leaves from the trees will provide longevity!

No more will there be cardiologist performing stress tests and placing stents in the coronary arteries, prescribing a handful of medications to prolong your life... with potentially nasty side effects! No more hospitals to tend to traumas, heart attacks, and cancer. No more urgent cares, emergency rooms, or intensive care units to tend to the sick! Just take a hold of the leaves from the trees! Eat! Enjoy! Laugh! Leap! Live! Live long! Live strong!

III. Heaven Eternal

From the End of the Milennium throughout All
Eternity

Born Twice.
Die Once.

After the Millennium ends, God will release Satan from the bottomless pit for a brief period. Satan will deceive a portion of the children of the "sheep" and the Jewish remnant that have not yet received their glorified bodies (Rev. 20:7–8). Unbelievable! In the most perfect environment, people still long to sin, and will reject Christ and desire to rebel against Him. Will the pundits be able to blame society, culture, or one's socioeconomic background? No, the problem lies in mankind's heart which is filled with selfishness, greed, and pride. During the Millennium, those who were not raptured may bow their knee to Christ, but not their hearts, because they will still be operating with a free will, making individual choices in a thousand-year era where righteousness is administered and mandated by the redeemed. We, the redeemed, who were given our glorified bodies cannot sin or be deceived by Satan.

Bowing the knee involuntarily is not the same as bowing the heart in humility. Once Satan is released, he will deceive the masses who never bowed their hearts to Christ, and they will follow the deceiver to Jerusalem to attack the city and attempt to dethrone Christ. This battle is also known as the "Gog and Magog" battle, yet it is not the actual Gog and Magog War that occurs right after the rapture. The final "Gog and Magog" battle is fought in the "spirit" of the real Gog and Magog War (Rev. 20:8). Satan will be stopped! Satan will be defeated! And he will finally be cast into hell, the Lake of Fire, joining the Antichrist and the False Prophet. Contrary to what many believe, Satan will not rule hell; he will be tormented in hell!

After the "Gog and Magog" battle, we will witness the most tragic of all events. An event that cannot be postponed any further. It cannot be delayed. It cannot be suspended. It cannot be extended or regarded as "continuance." This experience will occur in the third heaven. It is hair-raising! Horrendous! Heart-wrenching! It is the most tragic court appearance ever recorded in history of mankind!

At the end of the Millennium and the last battle of Gog and Magog, the bodies of all the dead in all of history who rejected God, His Son and the Holy Spirit, will come to life, known as the "Second Resurrection." Every single individual who rejected Christ will finally receive his eternal body, and that renewed body will unite with its soul and spirit from hades when entering the throne of heaven. Each person will then face God at the Great White Throne Judgment (Rev. 20:11). There will be no second chances. There will be no loopholes or appeals. There will be no bribery. There will be no parole. There will be no way out!

God will open the Book of Life, in which their names will not be found. The chronicles of books on each individual, which contain every thought, speech, and action, will then be opened. Every motive will be exposed. The people may protest that they were good citizens, that they were philanthropists, that they did not commit murder, and that they were kind neighbors. God will point to His Son who died on the cross of Calvary, illustrating that His Son is the only One good enough to atone for sin. God will then render to each person according to his deeds (Prov. 24:12; Rom. 2:1–11; Rev. 22:12). Heartbreaking!

These souls will tragically be cast into hell, the Lake of Fire, where there will be gnashing of teeth; where the worm will not die; where there will be agony upon agony without relief; and where the presence of God will be absent. Being cast into outer darkness, the Lake of Fire, is known as the "Second Death." It will be a place of utter misery, eternal punishment, dying eternally with a living conscience, and a living body, where all hope will be absent and the absence of God will be physically, psychologically, emotionally, and eternally tangible... forever! (Matt. 8:12; 13:40–42, 50; 22:13; 24:51; 25:30).

Those who died once but were born twice, first at birth and second through the redeeming blood of Jesus Christ, will not face God at the Great White Throne Judgment nor will they be "rewarded" with the Second Death. Those who were born only once and rejected the cleansing fountain of life, Jesus Christ, will die twice, first physically and then spiritually. Let's be clear. The Second Death is eternal death, with physical, emotional and spiritual agony upon agony. It is torment without breathing. It is sickness without healing. It is darkness without seeing. It is hopelessness without hoping. It is death without dying.

Today is the day of choosing! If you are not sure whether your name is written in the Book of Life, come to the cross of Calvary, accept Christ as your Savior and be born again! Why can we trust Him? Because He loves us as we are...while we were sinners, Christ died for us! (Rom. 5:8).

Why Christ? Why not any god? Why not any religion? The difference between Christianity and religion is simple:

1. All religions ask you to come up to a level of a god, please him, do good, and desperately hope that you will one day go to heaven if you have been "good enough." Only in Christianity do you have God coming down to us, knowing we are not able to come up to His holy level. God sent His only Son, Jesus Christ, to die for our sins, in our place as our substitutionary sacrifice, and offer us wholeness in Him that gives us a full assurance that we are going to heaven. "He who believes in the Son (Jesus Christ) has everlasting life. He who does not believe the Son shall not see life, but the wrath of God abides on him" (John 3:36). "Most assuredly, I say to you, he who hears My (Jesus') word and believes in Him (God) who sent Me has everlasting life, and shall not come into judgment, but has passed from death into life" (John 5:24). Only in Christ, can you be sure that you will be going to heaven!

2. All religions have rules that people must follow a god who is far off; Christ followers have fellowship with the Father, walking hand-in-hand with

Jesus Christ, and flourishing in the power of the Holy Spirit who lives within them.

3. In all religions, one must save himself. Only Christianity has the Savior, Jesus Christ, our Lord, our Redeemer, our salvation, and our hope!

4. Religion will make you go from the east to the west to find a way to rid yourself of your sins and guilty conscience. Jesus will make you a new creation and will completely cleanse you of all your sins and guilt as far as the east is from the west (Ps. 103:12). Fellowship with Him is incomprehensible: sins forgiven, sins forgotten, completely acquitted, and guilt eliminated!

5. To make it clear, imagine that you are stuck in a deep pit. Religion will throw you a rope and ask you to climb up, but there is no one on the other side to hold the rope and hoist you up. Christ, on the other hand, not only hands you the rope, but He pulls you up with all darkness, sin, and guilt left behind! Hallelujah to the Lamb of God! Praises to His name! Glory and honor belong to Him alone!

2 8

Custom-Built

Once the Millennium ends and judgments are decreed at the Great White Throne, the third heaven and earth will pass away (Rev. 21:1). Why would God get rid of heaven? He is not getting rid of heaven; He is getting rid of the third heaven. Satan desecrated its splendor; he was kicked out of heaven when he tried to ascend above God's throne (Isa. 14:11–15). He has been accusing the redeemed day and night for centuries and will continue to do so until the middle of the tribulation, when he will permanently be kicked out of heaven (Rev. 12:7–12). Why would God get rid of the earth? Because it is infested with pride, greed, sin, sickness, and death.

The psalmist proclaimed of God, "Of old, You laid the foundation of the earth. And the heavens are the work of Your hands. They will perish, but You will endure; yes, they will all grow old like a garment; like a cloak, You will change them and they will be changed. But

You are the same, and Your years will have no end" (Ps. 102:25–27).

After the Great White Throne Judgment, the redeemed will live forever in the "fourth" or eternal heaven. Since there will no longer be a third heaven, where will heaven be? The new heaven, called the new Jerusalem, the very same one that the Great Carpenter, our Savior, has been working on for two thousand years, will descend and rest upon the new earth. Jesus told us in John 14:2–3 that in His Father's house are mansions and He is preparing our eternal abode, customized, authorized, and the right size!

What will happen to the sun, the moon, and the stars? What will happen to our universe? We have a shadow, a glimpse, a peek of what the first and second heaven will be like, found in Revelation 22:5, "There shall be no night there (in the fourth heaven, the new Jerusalem). They need no lamp nor light of the sun, for the Lord God gives them (believers) light. And they shall reign forever and ever."

Paul tells us in Hebrews 12:22–24, "But you have come to Mount Zion and to the city of the living God, the heavenly Jerusalem, to an innumerable company of angels, to the general assembly and church of the firstborn who are registered in heaven, to God the Judge of all, to the spirits of just men made perfect, to Jesus the Mediator of the new covenant and to the blood of sprinkling that speaks better things than that of Abel."

We are going to dwell eternally in the New City of the living God with a perfect design and unimagined blessings, accompanied by countless angels, their numbers like the stars in the sky! We will also be surrounded by just neighbors, refined in Christ's righteousness, and in the presence of our compassionate and loving God, whose face we shall see! We will live in perfect provision, perfect love, perfect peace, perfect joy, perfect health, perfect purity, and perfect harmony. No evil hands that molest. No evil feet that chase. No evil hearts that hate. Just the redeemed, made perfect in Christ! Oh, how wonderful. Oh, how marvelous! Oh, how glorious!

We read in Revelation 21:9–12, "Come, I (an angel) will show you the bride, the Lamb's wife. And he carried me (John) away in the Spirit to a great and high mountain, and showed me the great city, the holy Jerusalem, descending out of heaven from God, having the glory of God. Her light was like a most precious stone, like a jasper stone, clear as crystal. Also, she had a great and high wall with twelve gates, and twelve angels at the gates, and names written on them, which are the names of the twelve tribes of the children of Israel."

According to Revelation 21:14, 19–21, there will be twelve foundations adorned with twelve brilliant stones, with each foundation bearing the name of one of Christ's twelve apostles. The twelve gates will be twelve pearls, and each individual gate of one pearl, and the street of the city will be pure gold like transparent glass.

The new Jerusalem will be 1,500 miles in length, 1,500 miles in width, and 1,500 miles in height (Rev. 21:16). One of the tallest buildings in the world, Burj Khalifa, in Dubai, United Arab Emirates, stands at 2,717 feet, approximately one-half of a mile high. A straight-line distance from Virginia to Colorado is approximately 1,500 miles. Can we even begin to comprehend a 1,500-mile-high, 1,500-mile-long, and a 1,500-mile-wide structure? No force except God could create such splendor, and no force will be able to topple His treasure.

The city is holy. It is filled with God's glory. Its lights shine brightly. Its foundations glitter with stones of beauty. Its twelve large gates are pearly. Its streets are pure gold, glistening brilliantly. There is the absence of adversity, impurity, immorality, and iniquity. Its very heart beats with tranquility! And it is our home sweet home for eternity!

What else is there to say?

TGIH! Yes, yes, yes! Thank God It's Heaven!

Bright Sunshiny Day

In Revelation 21:22–27 we read, "But I saw no temple in it, for the Lord God Almighty and the Lamb are its temple. The city had no need of the sun or for the moon to shine in it; for the glory of God illuminated it. The Lamb is its light. And the nation of those who are saved shall walk in its light, and the kings of the earth bring their glory and honor into it. Its gates shall not be shut at all by day (there shall be no night there). And they shall bring the glory and the honor of the nation into it. But there shall by no means enter it anything that defiles, or causes an abomination or a lie, but only those who are written in the Lamb's Book of Life."

There will be a temple built in the present-day Jerusalem during the tribulation (Rev. 11:1). There will be a temple during the Millennium in the new and renovated city of Jerusalem (Ezek. 41–47). But there will be no temple in the new heaven, the new Jerusalem! No structure. No building. No bricks. No entry from the east. No veil to cover or "hide" God's presence. No formalities. No pews. No podiums. No sacrifices. No bleeding lambs. No First Baptist. No Second Baptist. No Nazarene. No Presbyterian. No Methodist. No Assembly of God. No Pentecostal. No Evangelical. No denomination. No megachurches. No synagogues. For the Father, the Son and the Holy Spirit, as one, are the very temple in perfection.

Come! Come, all believers! Come, all those who are bought by the blood of the Lamb! Come, all those whose names are written in the Lamb's Book of Life. Come, all who have been given an eternal pardon! Come, for those upon whom God has declared, "Not guilty." Come, with full devotion. Come, with full joy. Come, and rest in the glory of the living God!

John writes in Revelation 22:1–2, "And he showed me a pure river of water of life, clear as crystal, proceeding from the throne of God and of the Lamb. In the middle of its street, and on either side of the river was the Tree of Life, which bore twelve fruits, each tree yielding its fruit every month. The leaves of the tree were for the healing of the nations."

There are many significant trees in the Bible. One that comes to mind is the Tree of Life in the Garden of Eden, which will reappear in eternity. Between the two events, the end of the beginning (Garden of Eden) and the beginning of the endless (new Jerusalem) there stands the cross, the tree that bore Christ on the hill of Calvary giving us life eternal as we trust in His redemptive work (Isa. 53:5–7; Acts 10:38–43; Gal. 3:13).

There will be no tree of the knowledge of good and evil to test us, for the former things including pain, sorrow, temptation, sin, and death will have passed away (Rev. 21:4). God will make all things new (Rev. 21:5). The Tree of Life in eternity will be nourished by the pure water of life that flows from God's throne. Its fruit will nourish us, and it leaves will be therapeutic...not to remedy sickness...as there is no sickness...but to quicken our hearts and energize our bodies. Amazing! From life, God Himself, flows living waters, which nourish the Tree of Life, which gives life to the redeemed forever and ever.

We read in Revelation 22:3–4, "And there shall be no more curse, but the throne of God and the Lamb shall be in it, and His servants shall serve Him. They shall see His face, and His name shall be on their foreheads." How beautiful! No one can upset you. No one can hurt you. No one can trick you. No one can trip you. No one can embarrass you. No one can belittle you. No one can leave you. No one can curse you. The throne of God, Christ and the Holy Spirit is accessible! The grace and beauty of God will be upon us! Believers will see God, serve God, and shine like the stars in the presence of God! (Dan. 12:3).

According to Revelation 22:5, "There shall be no night there (new Jerusalem): they need no lamp nor light of the sun, for the Lord God gives them light. And they shall reign forever and ever." Jesus said that He is the Light of the World and those who walk in Him shall have the light of life (John 8:12). In Revelation 1:16, Christ's countenance is like the sun that shines in all its strength. Do you recall seeing Christ walking with Shadrach, Meshach, and Abednego in the fiery furnace? According to King Nebuchadnezzar, "Look, I see four men loose, walking in the midst of the fire; and they are not hurt, and the form of the fourth is like the Son of God" (Dan. 3:25). Yes, our Christ outshines the darkness. Our Christ outshines your impossibilities. Our Christ outshines your trials! Our Christ outshines your worries! Our Christ outshines the fire! Our Christ outshines the sun! Our Christ outshines eternity!

3 0

No X, Y, Z

We are so accustomed to life as we know it today, entrenched in our activities, hiding our insecurities and preparing for the uncertainties. Can you imagine an entirely different way of living and loving? "And God will wipe away every tear from their eyes; there shall be no more death, nor sorrow, nor crying. There shall be no more pain, for the former things shall pass away. Then He who sat on the throne said, 'Behold, I make all things new'" (Rev. 21:4–5).

New. As in no chemotherapy? As in no medications? As in no incarceration? As in no loss? As in no loneliness? As in no psychiatric wards? As in no wars? As in no murder? As in no ethnic cleansing? As in no genocides? As in no terrorism? As in no nuclear threat? As in no hospitals? As in no rape? As in no divorce? As in no mistakes? As in no censorship? As in no tyranny? As in no cruelty? As in no bullying? As in no poverty? As in no child abuse? As in no abortions? As in no suicide? Yes, none of these toxic conditions! Heaven is all happy. All joyful. All delightful. All hopeful. All rejoicing. All laughter. All worship. All heartening. All restful. All peaceful. All positive. All good. All day long. For all eternity...we will live in happily forever after!

Finally! We shall experience heaven on earth!

No addiction, no affliction, no adversaries, no aging.

No betraying, no belittling, no bitterness, no breaking.

No commotion, no confusion, no cruelty, no crying.

No depression, no disease, no disappointments, no dying.

No enmity, no errors, no evil, no envying.

No filth, no falsehood, no falling, no failing.

No gimmicks, no gloom, no grudges, no gossiping.

No harassment, no hopelessness, no hate, no harming.

No immorality, no indifference, no injustice, no ill-being.

No jealousy, no junk, no jabbing, no jeering.

No kinks, no kickbacks, no kidnapping, no killing.

No lying, no loneliness, no losing, no lacking.

No malady, no misfortune, no misery, no mourning.

No nasty, no nightmare, no nagging, no neglecting.

No obscurity, no offense, no outcast, no overthrowing.

No pain, no panic, no pride, no persecuting.

No quacks, no quarrels, no quandaries, no quitting.

No rage, no rape, no rust, no rejecting.

No sin, no scam, no senility, no suffering.

No taxes, no threats, no trouble, no taunting.

No unclean, no unfairness, no upset, no usurping.

No vulgarity, no vengeance, no villain, no vexing.

No wrong, no woe, no whining, no worrying.

No X.

No Y.

No Z.

And that's just the beginning of this grace-filled story!

Yes! Yes! Sing praises to our Lord Jesus Christ!

Dance light-heartedly!

Sing joyfully!

Shout emphatically!

"TGIH!"

"Thank God It's Heaven!"

Fast Pass to Disneyland

Have you ever been to Disneyland, the "happiest place on earth?" If you were to look around, you would easily spot children who do not look anything close to being "happy!" Some of the yelling and screaming you hear is not coming from the rides...but from the mouths of the "happy" children throwing a fit!

Heaven, on the other hand, is by far the happiest place! The glory of the new Jerusalem is not its sparkling walls, its pearly doors, or its golden streets and floors. It is not in its angels bowing before the Lord God, cherubim worshiping Him or the redeemed with our glorified bodies. It is not found in the magnitude and architecture of the new Jerusalem. It is not in its brilliant foundations of jasper, sapphire, chalcedony, emerald, sardonyx, sardius, chrysolite, beryl, topaz, chrysoprase, jacinth, nor amethyst.

The splendor of heaven is its center of attraction: God, Christ, and the Holy Spirit in its midst! The triune Almighty God! No matter how spectacular the new heaven will appear, communing with the Lord face to face will be in and of itself the most beautiful habitation of all! We will gaze upon the beauty of the Lord and be known by His name. For those who do not like their names, there is hope! According to Revelation 2:17, all of us will be given a brand-new name by Christ, only known to the one who receives it!

King David anticipated seeing the Lord face to face, as he sang in Psalm 27:4, "One thing I have desired of the Lord, this will I seek: that I may dwell in the house of the Lord all the days of my life, to behold the beauty of the Lord and to seek Him in His temple." What are we longing for? What does this world have to offer us? At the end of the day, everything on earth is temporary and empty. Why? Because God has placed eternity in our hearts and nothing in this world will be able to fill it or satisfy it! (Ecc. 3:11).

In Psalm 73:25–26, King David spoke to us about the importance of a life committed to the Lord, "Whom have I in heaven but You? And there is none upon earth that I desire besides You. My flesh and my heart fail but God is the strength of my heart and my portion forever." The time spent with the Lord, meditating on the Word of the Lord, and serving the Lord on earth stamp out fear, doubt and unbelief, and are the greatest benchmarks of our longing for heaven!

Take a thorough inventory of your life today. Be realistic. What do you delight in the most? What is the greatest desire of your heart? What will you do with all the stuff you collected?

You can have the mansions of this world; you can have its glittering lights; you can have its delicacies; its wineries; its degrees; its follies; its monies; its parties; its worries; its dynasties; its fantasies; its industries; its melodies; its remedies; its difficulties; its securities; its utilities; its philosophies; its possibilities; its apostasies; and its celebrities. All of it. You can have all of it, and then some.

Just give me Jesus!
Just give me Jesus!
Just give me Jesus!

From Glory to Glory

Heaven is not that we will solely be with the Father. Heaven is that the Father will be with us! There are no legal issues. No prosecution. No defense. No verdict. No sentence. There are no health issues. No illness. No diagnosis. No treatment. No prognosis. None of these tribulations can exist in the presence of our Father. He is our God. He is our friend. He is our Papa. He is our defense. He is our Advocate. He is our Great Physician. Forever we are guiltless! Forever we are whole! And we are His children, the sheep of His pasture. We are His beloved, held closely to His bosom (Isa. 40:11).

What will happen to us in heaven? We will go from glory to glory. We will fly from galaxy to galaxy. We will reach from height to height. We will soar from grace to grace. We will enjoy blessings upon blessings. We will experience goodness upon goodness. We will have riches upon riches. We will smile from hope to hope. We will rejoice from joy to joy. We will relish in God's mercies upon mercies. We will be strengthened from health to health. We will be comforted from peace to peace. We will live endlessly from eternity to eternity!

The redeemed will not be crying. We will not be aging. We will not be hurting. We will not be fearing. We will not be worrying. We will not be dying. We will be dancing. We will be laughing. We will be celebrating. We will be worshiping. We will be serving. We will be enjoying. Like heaven's stars, we will be shining. We will forever be in a state of perfect living!

Wipe away our tears, Lord. Cast away death, Lord. Stamp out sorrow, Lord. End our worries, Lord. Take away all our pain, Lord. The former things have passed away! The new has come!

All things new...forever.
All things new...no more Satan, the accuser.
All things new...no more guilt and dishonor.
All things new...in the sweet arms of our Savior! (Rev. 21:4–5).

Sing glory, power, and praises to our Lord.
Sing unto our Lord a new song.
Sing, dance and shout, "Glory, glory, hallelujah."
Sing, "Great is our Lord for all eternity long!"

Headaches will be gone.
Heartaches cannot be.
Harm will cease.
Honor for all eternity!

Yes! Yes!
Shout it from the mountain tops! Shout it again and again!
"TGIH!"
"Thank God It's Heaven!"

Twice Victorious

"Surely I am coming quickly" is the last declaration made by Jesus Christ at the end of the book of Revelation (Rev. 22:20). Yes, He is coming speedily, suddenly, and swiftly!

Allow me to ask you a couple of questions before you finish this book. What kind of decisions are you making today that will affect your eternity? And where will you end up after the grave? How will your benefits here on earth compare to the benefits you will receive after your last breath?

I asked these questions to one of my recent patients, Steve, as I visited him in the intensive care unit. I had performed a stress test on him four months earlier. Though he did not have any chest pains, there were significant electrocardiogram changes which concerned me. After the testing, I strongly advised Steve to have an angiogram; he adamantly refused. Why? Because he did not have any symptoms and he said, "I just don't need it, Doc; I feel good." After several attempts at describing the consequences of not doing the test, I honored my patient's wishes because it is unethical to coerce him or anyone to undergo a procedure.

Four months later he was on his home treadmill working out when he collapsed. His daughter found her father on the floor, face down. In horror, she turned him over on his back but could not awaken him. She felt for his pulse; none was present. CPR was started and 911 was called. Paramedics arrived and found him to be in ventricular fibrillation, a rhythm that is incompatible with life. They shocked him out of death and placed a tube through the mouth to help him breathe.

When he arrived at the hospital, we artificially chilled his body to slow down his metabolism in hopes of preserving his brain function because no one knew how long he was without oxygen. A ventilator assisted his breathing. He had a major heart attack while working out that caused the electrical upheaval in his heart, leading to a sudden cardiac arrest.

There was talk among the doctors that if he were to wake up, he would be in a vegetative state. When I heard that, I prayed over him, stating, "In the name of Jesus, Steve you will wake up!" After pouring in medications in his frail veins and, more importantly, praying for complete recovery in the name of Jesus Christ, our patient came to seventy-two hours later by God's grace. When the ventilator was removed, he was alert, awake, oriented, and defeatedly not a vegetable!

I then performed the angiogram. There was a 90 percent blockage in his left main artery, the key "freeway" that gives life to all the significant "freeways" on the left side of the heart. The arteries on the left each had 99 percent blockages. The right artery was 100 percent blocked. The fact that he was alive meant that he beat 100 percent odds! The fact that he was fully functional mentally meant that God had intervened in saving him! Because there were too many blockages to be stented, he underwent a bypass surgery and did exceptionally well. He now walks five miles a day and takes good care of his body.

I had spoken to Steve about Christ and His offer of salvation in the past. I asked him if he knew where he was going when he died, heaven or hell, and if his name was written in the Lamb's Book of Life. He was not sure. I shared with him the beauty of Christ and how much He loved him. Then I asked him if he would accept Him. Steve's tender heart said, "Yes!" In that moment we prayed together, and Steve accepted Jesus Christ as His Savior and Lord. He was saved not only physically, but also spiritually! Not only does he have new freeways in his heart to give him a new start, but now, his name is written in the Lamb's Book of Life to give him eternal life! Alive physically. Alive spiritually! Living twice, victoriously!

My heart rejoices for Steve; yet my heart grieves for Jim, my patient whom we met in chapter one, who refused to go to the hospital and died at home. He adamantly refused to accept the Lord. Dead physically. Dead Spiritually. Dying twice, eternally.

How about you? How is your physical heart? More importantly, how is your spiritual heart? Is it in atrial fibrillation? Is it in ventricular fibrillation? Is your name written in the Lamb's Book of Life? Where will you go after the grave? How sure are you? This is not a decision about buying a car or a house; it is not about what you wear or what you eat; it is not about holding the mayonnaise or pouring on the ketchup; this is the most critical decision of your life; a decision that will permanently establish your eternal destiny.

Will you consider Christ's love, forgiveness, and blessings for you and upon you?

If you are in your youth, you may say you have plenty of time.

If you are in your early adulthood, you may say you are hard at work.

If you are in your middle adulthood, you may say you are on the move and will consider it later.

If you are in your later adulthood, you may say you are too busy planning for your retirement.

If you are elderly, you may say that your senses are too diminished to grasp the truth.

When one dies, there is nothing else to say. No excuses. No rebuttals. No more opportunities.

Jesus has given His life for you. He is not a program; He is a person. He is not a natural man; He is the supernatural Son of Man, the Son of God. He is not a way; He is the only Way. He is not a god; He is God, the second person of the Trinity. He has paved the way for you to live a life of eternal goodness in heaven, where there will be no more pain, no more sorrow, no more tears, no more loss, no more separation, and no more death.

Won't you come? Today is your day of salvation! Come and lay your weary soul at the cross of the Lamb! Come and forever have your name written in the Lamb's Book of Life. Come and enjoy a life of abundance, free of guilt, free of oppression, and free of lack. When you come as you are, He accepts you as you are; in fact, He knew you and loved you before you were even born! (Jer. 1:5).

The darkness of this age will be pierced. Jesus is coming back...soon! Are you ready? Are you sure you are going to heaven? When you accept the only treatment for your weary soul and spirit, the blood of Christ, you will be cured of your "spiritual" atrial fibrillation and ventricular fibrillation, you will walk in rhythm with God, you will experience heaven on earth, your name will be written in the Lamb's Book of Life, and you will live in heaven forever.

What a happy day that will be when my Jesus I shall see! We, the redeemed, will be dancing our hearts out on streets of gold!

Sing with all your heart!
Shout with all your might!
Proclaim it over and over!
"TGIH!"
Amen and amen!
"Thank God It's Heaven!"

IV. Heaven Bound

From Now through Eternity

Heaven, Yes

No one, including Peter the apostle, will be at the pearly gates asking you what the password is to get into heaven. No one will be asking you, "Why should I let you into heaven?" If you are looking for the only "password," it should have been accessed here on earth, on Calvary's hill, in humility, under the blood of Jesus Christ.

We find in God's Word that all of us have sinned and all of us have fallen short of the glory of God, leading us to a state of spiritual death and eternal damnation (Rom. 3:23; 6:23). The cross of Calvary, where Jesus the Son of God shed His blood, forms the bridge, a sweet fellowship, between a holy God and unholy people. Jesus is the only way to heaven. All other roads and bridges lead to hell (Acts 4:12; John 3:36).

Many people believe they are good. Good deeds, good morals, good behavior, and the lack of bad deeds will not get anyone into heaven! Billions believe that they must earn their way into heaven by working, praying and serving. Satan is not opposed to your good morals and good conduct. He is opposed to Jesus Christ! Why? Because there is only one good, Jesus Christ. There is only one work, Jesus Christ's complete work on the cross, that will grant a soul access into heaven.

I'm sure you have heard the saying, "Well, I'm not as bad as that person!" The only comparison game is our imperfect works compared to Jesus' perfect work. Our works lead us to death. Jesus' work leads us to eternal life. Once we admit that we are sinners and accept the cleansing power of the blood of the Lamb, we can begin experiencing the joys of heaven…even while we are on earth! It is only after receiving the cleansing power of Jesus' blood that our works, done out of love for our Lord, have eternal value.

It is tragic to witness that many Christ followers believe that Satan is all powerful. Adam and Eve were given the kingdom authority of heaven and dominion over all the earth until Satan usurped their power by deceiving them. Christ died on the cross and rose from the dead to break Satan's grip, but most Christ followers are oblivious about their righteous standing and towering authority. If Christ, who lives in us, is greater than Satan (1 John 4:4), and He is, then why do we operate in fear? If the same resurrection power that raised Christ from the dead is in us (Eph.1:18–20), and it is, why do we walk in doubt, speak in unbelief, and act in desperation? When believers watch and listen to the same junk that the world views and hears, we lack biblical knowledge, compromise our convictions, and lose our commitment to Christ.

If one has to be perfect to get to heaven, then none of us can join the party. But there is hope! The Holy Spirit leads us to the Way! When we accept Christ as our Savior and Lord, we are made perfect, whole, and righteous in Him (2 Cor. 5:21). We are made sons and daughters of our heavenly Father. We are made warriors, fueled by the power of the Holy Spirit. We become royal, priests, and God's own special people! And when this short life is over, we will be accepted into heaven...what a day of rejoicing that will be!

Eternity with Christ! Truly, we will be singing, dancing, and shouting, "TGIH! Thank God It's Heaven!" But what about now? What about our lives in this broken world? Today, we are triumphant in Christ! How so? The salvation of Jesus not only saves us from eternal hell, but heals us currently, literally and physically. Salvation frees us from all oppression, depression, and demonic strongholds; and salvation drastically changes our pauper-minded disposition. "TGIH!" can start today in your life!

When the eyes of our understanding become enlightened, we will know the hope of our calling, the riches of the glory of our inheritance, the greatness of God's power within us...the same power that raised Christ from the dead! (Eph. 1:18–20). According to Ephesians 2:6, those who believe and are committed to Christ "sit together in the heavenly places in Christ," today, even in our day-to-day lives! Once we realize the great riches Christ has given us, we will also begin living in the assurance of Ephesians 3:20, which states that our heavenly Father is able to do "exceedingly abundantly above all that we ask or think, according to the power that works in us."

We are victorious! We are a chosen generation! We are a royal priesthood! We are a holy nation! We are God's own people! We can and should enjoy heaven's beauty today on earth! Satan can't have us. He can't have our minds. He can't have our bodies. He can't have his way! We allow our own pride, our own lusts, our own fears, our own wills, and our own ignorance to get in the way of enjoying heaven today! The antidote is simple: we are to thirst for God's Word and allow the Word to renew our minds and transform our lives. Spending time with

Christ and in His Word will bring wisdom into our lives, health to our bodies, transformation to our minds, strength to our weaknesses, and hope in the midst of our fears.

There are not many roads to heaven...Jesus is the only way to heaven. The current heaven is at the farthest north and is inhabited by God, Jesus, the Holy Spirit, angels, and believers who have gone before us. It is a place of joy, a place of wellness, and a place of eternal security. Despite its beauty, the current heaven will pass away, and a new heaven, called the new Jerusalem, will be established on the new earth, 1,007 years after the rapture.

In the rapture, Christ will come to take believers up to heaven to live with Him. A seven-year period of tribulation will follow on earth, culminating in the Second Coming of Christ and the campaign of Armageddon. Christ will then rule on earth for a thousand years with His saints, the believers. After the thousand years, Satan will launch his final and futile rebellion, and be cast into hell. Unbelievers of all time will be judged at the Great White Throne and be sentenced to hell. And then...the new heaven will descend on the new earth in timeless eternity, and believers will enjoy the glory of the living God forever!

The gift of God, His Son, Jesus Christ the Lord, gives us hope, peace, and wholeness, and leads to eternal life, eternal goodness, eternal joy, and eternal liberty. Believers will live eternally with our Lord, basking in His beauty, and enjoying life as it was meant to be...in perfect rest, perfect peace, and perfect love forever and ever! Amen!

Hell, No

Hell was never intended to be inhabited by human be-ings. There is currently no one "living" in the pits of hell. According to Matthew 25:41, hell was prepared for Satan, the rebellious archangel, and his demons. It is a place of outer darkness, burning with sulfur, tears, fears, and everlasting agony. There will be a lot of good people in hell. Being good does not exempt one from going to hell.

Jesus paid a price on the cross of Calvary that we could not pay. We were born in sin and the penalty or wages of sin is death (Rom. 6:23). Christ took on our sins and our death and became our substitutionary sacrifice by shedding His blood and cancelling our sin debt (John 3:16–17; Heb. 9:22). When He rose from the dead on the third day, He set the stage for us to escape the clutches of hell, but only if we accept His atoning blood for our sins (Acts 4:12). Those who have died rejecting Christ are currently in a horrible holding area called hades. Hades will spew forth all the dead who died without Christ into the presence of God at the Great White Throne after the Millennium Era, where they will be judged, sentenced, and sent to hell.

Why does Satan continue to oppress and deceive people? I am convinced that he knows his end, and he hates people so much that he wants them to join him in his ultimate demise. He paints rebellion on an attractive canvas of power, prestige and popularity, but blinds the masses to reality of their destination: the pits of hell.

Hell is eternal. It is a place of gnashing teeth, sorrow, death without dying, torture without stopping, and agony without ending. It will be the habitation of everyone who rejects Christ. God does not want anyone to perish but that everyone come to repentance (Ezek. 33:11; 2 Peter 3:9); it is the individual who rejects God and chooses hell. It is Satan that fools the minds, blinds the eyes, and hardens the hearts of people, dragging them into hell because he hates mankind and wants us to suffer. Hell is not cool. It is not a fable. It is not filled with bars, pool tables, and golf courses. It is not a reprieve for those who choose to live life their own way. It is eternal torment. It is the greatest tragedy known to mankind because it never ends!

If you don't believe in hades and hell, all you have to do is wait one split second after you die. After death, you will face the horrid reality, and then, you will believe. But then, sadly, it will be too late.

Choose today whom you will serve!

God or Satan.

Choose today where you will live eternally!

Heaven or hell.

It all comes down to one choice...you either do it your way or God's way.

Backstage Passes and Comback Prayers

There are two eternal destinations: heaven or hell. The loving and compassionate heart of our Lord Jesus does not want anyone to perish in hell (Ezekiel 18:23; 1 Timothy 2:4; 2 Peter 3:9). We read in Isaiah 30:18 that the Lord is both gracious and compassionate. The admission process for heaven cannot be rigged or earned; it was bought for you and me by the sacrifice of Jesus on the cross.

According to Psalm 73:19, 24, those who reject God's gift of salvation, no matter what their status is, will plummet into desolation and destruction in a split moment, and will utterly be consumed with terrors in eternal hell. But those who love Christ will not only enjoy God's guidance and goodness in the land of the living, but will one day be received into God's amazing glory.

We have been given a backstage pass to enter into God's glory. He has filled out the entire application for us, line by line, and sealed our documents with the blood of the Lamb. Though my medical school application was based on my merit, my entrance into heaven is based on the perfect works of Christ alone. It is our choice to write our own story and live our lives as it pleases us by filling out our own applications, with our own strength, our own ability, our own agenda, and our own wits. God will always respect our free will to choose. He has given us the privilege to decide, to accept or reject Jesus. That one decision will not only direct our paths, but it will settle our eternal destiny...forever.

God has given us the Bible, His Word, churches, evangelists, and Christian media outlets. Those who read this book have been prayed for by a team of loving Christians! You may even have believing members of your family who are praying for you this moment so that you may come to Christ. How glorious it will be to meet one another in heaven! You may be asking yourself, "So how do I choose Jesus and heaven? I want to be certain in my heart that I'm going to heaven and that one sweet day, I'll be singing, 'TGIH! Thank God It's Heaven!'" Romans 10:9–11 makes it clear, "That if you confess with your mouth the Lord Jesus and believe in your heart that God has raised Him from the dead, you will be saved.

For with the heart one believes unto righteousness, and with the mouth, confession is made unto salvation. For the Scripture says, 'Whoever believes on Him will not be put to shame.'"

I should caution you, however, about the word, "believe." According to James 2:19, "You believe that there is one God. You do well. Even the demons believe—and tremble!" Believing is not a causal verbal pledge. Believing is committing your life to Christ.

Tomorrow? No. You don't have tomorrow. According to Hebrews 3:7, 15 and 4:7, today is the day of your salvation! A sudden cardiac arrest, like what occurred in my patient's life, will not give you that one second you hoped for. While you are alive, while you are breathing, while your faculties are intact, come! Come and hand in your admission papers, signed by the blood of the Lamb, and hand them over, along with your repentant heart, to the living God!

You may say that you don't want to hand your admission papers to God because you want to be in control. That's a choice you make...as long as you understand that if you don't hand over your admission papers to God, you've already handed them over to Satan!

To make your application for heaven complete, simply come, kneel at the cross, and allow the blood of Jesus at Calvary's hill to cleanse you of your sins, transform your heart and mind in Christ, lift off oppression and set you on the road of joy, filled with the power of the Holy Spirit (Acts 2:38). Come as you are, so that you may receive Christ, and one day, attend class in the finest institution, eternal heaven!

Let's pray together...

Father, I thank you for the greatest gift in all eternity, your atoning blood that was shed specifically for me on the hill of Calvary. I was born in sin and have no means of saving myself. You sent Your only Son, Jesus Christ, to die for me on the cross. Jesus humbled Himself by becoming a man, endured Your just punishment that was meant for me, and accepted the wages of sin which is death. Jesus was my substitute. Jesus was the slain Lamb. Jesus is the resurrection who gives me eternal life!

Why would You take the blame for me? Because You love me! I dishonored You, yet You loved me. I rebelled against You, yet You came for me. Your blood has completely cleansed me. Clean! Clean! Forever I am clean and forgiven under the blood of the Lamb! Sinful no more! Guilty no more! I am greatly beloved by You!

The stripes Your Son took on His back have healed my body and freed my mind of oppression! Thank you for conquering sin, sickness, poverty, and death. I now belong to You. My name is etched forever in the Lamb's Book of Life, and I am certain that I will be with You for all of eternity, singing Your praises and living in the light of the risen Lamb!

According to Your Word in John 17:3, eternity is knowing You, the only true God. I thank You for the Holy Spirit who now resides in my heart and is my Advocate. Holy Spirit, lead me in the paths of life, teach me Your ways, quieten me with Your love, rejoice over me with singing, and lift me up day to day in Your power so that I may live victoriously! I will rejoice in You, love You, honor You, and live my life on earth with fullness of joy and in the abundance of Your mercy and goodness. In the name of Jesus I pray, amen and amen!

Books & Online

Other books by Dr. Sam

Playing on Your Last String
Mirror, Mirror on the Wall
Not on My Shift
I Got a Big But(t)
Absolute Hope
Life Prescriptions
Counting What Counts
Mad Love
When Hope Finds You
God Knows Your Address

Children's Books with CDs by Dr. Sam

Friends with Tommie Bear
Tommie Bear Goes to School

Revelation Series by Dr. Sam

Rev It Up - Verse by Verse (Volumes I and II)
Rev It Up - Step by Step (Chronological order)
Rev It Up - Rhyme by Rhyme (Poetry book)
Rev It Up - Image by Image (Illustrated book)
Rev It Up - for Kids (Children's book)
Rev It Up - Rap It Up (CD)

Dr. Sam Online

Web: BeaconOfHearts.org
       MenderOfHearts.org

YouTube: Dr. Samuel Kojoglanian

Instagram: @DrKojoglanian

Twitter: @BeaconOfHearts
          @MenderOfHearts

Facebook:
       BeaconOfHearts
       MenderOfHearts
       DrSam Kojoglanian

CPSIA information can be obtained
at www.ICGtesting.com
Printed in the USA
JSHW050138280722
28576JS00006B/95